Royal Priesthood Advancing the Kingdom of Heaven on Earth

KATHLEEN MARTINEZ

WESTBOW
PRESS®
A DIVISION OF THOMAS NELSON
& ZONDERVAN

WestBow Press books may be ordered through booksellers or by contacting:

WestBow Press
A Division of Thomas Nelson & Zondervan
1663 Liberty Drive
Bloomington, IN 47403
www.westbowpress.com
1 (866) 928-1240

ISBN: 978-1-9736-5081-2 (sc)
ISBN: 978-1-9736-5080-5 (e)

Print information available on the last page.

WestBow Press rev. date: 02/06/2019

Dedication:

To my husband Daniel Martinez, Dusty and
Rachel Robello, and Kellie Martinez

Table of Contents

In the Beginning – B'reshite[1]

Throughout history, humanity has gazed in awe upon the heavens, observing the solar system, and innumerable galaxies. Although the magnificent display of the heavenly bodies continues to give glory to their Creator, ungodly men deny His existence and reject His Sovereignty. Moreover, they worship the beauty and wonder of nature. Because of their unbelief, the wicked suppress the knowledge of God and are deceived by Satan. Therefore, humanity possesses a spirit of hostility and rebellion toward God. Nevertheless, the Lord extends His loving nature and goodness by placing eternity in their heart and conscience. In reality, they are like lost children suffering from a void and emptiness of their spirit, longing for an intimate relationship with God as their Father. In response to their inner cry to know him, the heavenly Father has revealed Himself and His plan of salvation to godly men. By faith, they have responded to His call to follow Him and obey His Voice. In a burning bush, God called out to Moses and revealed Himself as the Great "I am" who hears the cry of His people for deliverance from Egyptian slavery and oppression. In obedience to the call of God, Moses delivered the children of Israel to be a holy nation. Through performing great miracles, signs and wonders, God demonstrated His Lordship over the nations and in particular Israel. In the wilderness, the Lord declared Himself to be their God. Through the prophetic ministry of Moses, God revealed Himself as the Creator of the heavens and the earth. Moreover, as a royal priesthood, Israel is called to worship their Creator. The people who are called by His Name fear God as

---

[1] William J. Morford, *The One New Man Bible: Revealing Jewish Roots and Power* (Traveler's Rest, South Carolina: True Potential Publishing, Inc., 2011), 1.

their Creator and obey His commandments written in the Hebrew Bible.

"In the beginning God created the heavens and the earth". In Genesis, the book of the beginnings, God revealed Himself as the Creator of the universe. By faith, Jews and Christians hold firmly to their conviction that the Hebrew Bible presents the only true and reliable account of Creation. Moreover, "All Scripture is given by the inspiration of God and is profitable for doctrine, for reproof, for correction, and instruction in righteousness that the man of God may be complete, thoroughly equipped for every good work " (II Timothy 3:16). Furthermore, no prophecy of Scripture is of any private interpretation, " for prophecy never came by the will of men, but holy men of God spoke as they were moved by the Holy Spirit" (II Peter 1:20,21). Without the illumination of the Spirit of God, no man is able to interpret or understand the true meaning of God's Word. The Spirit of Truth imparts a "spirit of wisdom and revelation in the knowledge of Him, the eyes of your understanding being enlightened; that you may know what is the hope of His calling, what are the riches of the glory of His inheritance in the saints" (Ephesians 1:17, 18). In his letter to the Ephesians, Paul prayed that the spiritual eyes of the saints would be opened to receive a deeper personal knowledge and understanding of God. His earnest desire was to raise up church leadership (apostles, prophets, evangelists, pastors and teachers) "for the equipping of the saints of God, for the work of the ministry, for the edifying of the body of Christ" The role of church leaders was to train and prepare people for their particular service and ministry inside and outside the church to the end that all would "come into the unity of the faith and of the knowledge of the Son of God to a perfect man to the measure of the stature of Christ" (Ephesians 4:11-13) The spiritual growth of the church is measured by the overall conformity of her members to the image of Christ in His nature and character. To attain spiritual maturity, the children of God are to be diligent and disciplined in their daily study and application of the Word of God. "Be diligent to present yourself approved to God, a worker who does not need to be ashamed, rightly dividing the word of truth" (II Timothy 2:15).The day will surely arrive when all Christians will face judgment of God who will test the quality of their works by fire. If their works are deemed as worthless in the Kingdom of God, they will be burned as hay, wood, and stubble. Although they will not lose their salvation, they will stand before God ashamed of their works (I Corinthians 3:12-15). Therefore, the members of the church encourage one another to do good works and grow in their personal knowledge of Him. They speak "the truth in love that they may grow up in all things into Him...Christ" (Ephesians 4:15) By His Word, they are sanctified and set apart to be His inheritance in Christ through whom they have obtained His eternal life. In order to build a mature, godly character, Christians must fill their hearts and minds with the Word of Christ (Colossians 3:16). Empowered by the Spirit and the Word of God, they have the capacity and power to fulfill their calling in the Kingdom of God. Through the power and authority vested in the Name of the Lord Jesus Christ, Christians are called to rule and reign with Christ who is now seated at the right hand of God. Presently, He is held in the heavens until His enemies are totally decimated and put under His feet. (I Corinthians 15:25). "For He must reign till He has put all enemies under His Feet" (Psalm 110:1).

The challenge of this dissertation to all members of the Body of Christ is to grow up into full maturity in Christ, fulfill their calling to walk daily in His victory, and put Satan under their feet. Spiritual maturity is the inner strength and fortitude to stand against the evil forces. In the book of Revelation, the saints of God overcome all enemy forces by the Blood of the Lamb, the Word of God as their testimony, and the laying down of their lives (Revelation 12:11). As overcomers, they acquire skill in spiritual warfare through the exercising of their faith. Through intercession and prayer without ceasing, mighty men, women, and children penetrate the dark domain of Satan to destroy his evil works. Moreover, there is no age limit in the call to effective ministry and service unto God, the Father.

Furthermore, all Christians are called to be the light that shines in a dark world. Through signs, wonders, and miracles, they are able to demonstrate the power and presence of God's Kingdom. His people are called to reflect the glory of God through their daily walk. Their lives are a testimony of God's power to rule over all His enemies. Now, the saints of God must impact the culture of humanism that has stood in opposition to the Kingdom of God. The church must provide strong leaders who effectively expose and destroy corrupt men and women who seek to destroy the spiritual heritage of the United States of America. As the righteousness of God, spiritual leaders are to be bold and strong in their declaration of the truth of the Gospel. All Christians use their divine power and authority to defeat their enemies. Victory in Christ is assured for His overcomers, for He has established His church upon Himself as a firm foundation. He is the Rock upon which she stands. Therefore, the gates of Hell will not prevail against her. The risen Lord Jesus Christ, He poured out the Holy Spirit to empower His disciples as witnesses of His resurrection.

In His Upper Room Discourse, Jesus revealed to His disciples that He had many things to say to them. (John 16:7). The Holy Spirit would be sent by the Father to further instruct them in all the truth. On the day of His ascension to heaven, Jesus commanded His apostles to wait for the Baptism of the Holy Spirit, who would empower them to be His witnesses "in Jerusalem, all of Judea and Samaria and to the end of the earth" (Acts 1:8). Since the Day of Pentecost, the Spirit of Truth continues to be a dynamic spiritual force in the church. Today, the Spirit of God continues to embolden His disciples to fulfill the Great Commission in Matthew 28:18-20. "All power and authority has been given to Me (Christ) in heaven and earth. Go therefore and make disciples of all the nations".

Through His death and resurrection, Christ became the Lord and ruler over all nations on earth (Psalm 2:8). Through the work

Kathleen Martinez

of the cross, Christ created in Himself a new humanity (Ephesians 2:14-15). Now, the work of the Holy Spirit is to mold the "one new man" into conformity with the image of Christ (Romans 8:28, 29). As mature disciples, Christians reveal the compassionate nature and moral character of God. The indwelling Holy Spirit empowers them to perform great signs, miracles, and wonders that open the hearts of men to receive salvation and entrance into the Kingdom of God. As ambassadors of Christ, they are called to carry out His earthly ministry of reconciliation (II Corinthians 5:20). "Now then we are ambassadors as though God were pleading through us: we implore you on Christ's behalf, be reconciled to God for Christ". As envoys of Christ, they show through their works convincing evidence of the Father's love and forgiveness. The Lord Jesus is fulfilling His promise to be with them as they boldly preach the Good News of salvation and deliverance.

Moreover, as children of God, they live by faith pressing into the mark of the high calling of God in Christ Jesus. They must not allow anything to stop them from reaching their full maturity in Christ and fulfilling their work in the Kingdom of God. Daily prayer and Bible study is vital for their spiritual growth. As they devote their time in His Presence, they are transformed by the Spirit of God into the divine nature and character of Christ. As Christians gaze upon Him in praise and worship, they are changed from glory to glory. "Now the Lord is the Spirit and where the Spirit of the Lord is, there is liberty. But we all...beholding as in a mirror the glory of the Lord, are being transformed into the same image from glory to glory, just as by the Spirit of the Lord" (II Corinthians 3:17-18). Through His Word and His Spirit, God patiently works in the hearts and minds of His people, drawing them into a closer and a more intimate relationship with Him so that they become like a flawless mirror that reflects His glory and majesty. Thus, the Spirit of God imparts His mind, wisdom, strength, and counsel, so that the saints gain a true knowledge of the Father, Son, and Holy Spirit. Moreover, they know that in Christ, they are adopted sons and daughters of the

King. They stand before the throne of heaven as kings and priests, freely offering to Him their lives in His supernatural service. Sid Roth declares that all Christians are naturally supernatural.

The realm of the supernatural is the light that dispels the darkness on earth. Although conflicting ideologies continue to be the cause of ongoing wars, death, and destruction on earth, the promises in the Word of God brings humanity assurance and a living hope of everlasting peace and prosperity in His Kingdom both now and in the coming age. In the book of Revelation, God promises to create a new heaven and a new earth (Revelation 21:1). The Word of God provides His people hope of a bright future in His presence. As the children of God walk in the Light, they will not stumble in darkness. Knowing and obeying the Truth is their powerful weapon that causes them to triumph over the corruption of the world. In their faithfulness to God, they reject the lies of the Devil who is an impotent and defeated foe. Satan flees when he hears the children of God quoting His Word, praising His Name, and declaring the mighty works that He has done in their lives.

Throughout human history, God has made Himself known through His supernatural signs, miracles, and wonders on the behalf of Israel (Deuteronomy 4:32-35). In the book of Deuteronomy, Moses warned Israel not to forget their covenant with the Lord their God who is consuming fire. He is a jealous God (Deuteronomy 4:23, 24). "Take heed to yourselves, lest you forget the covenant of the Lord your God which He made with you and make for yourselves a carved image in the form of anything which the Lord you God has forbidden you". Clearly, He has strictly forbidden His people to make carved images and declares that He will not tolerate their worship of other gods. His consuming fire is His great love for His people, and His burning desire is that they remain loyal to Him in their service to Him. Through their full devotion and consecration as His special people, He is able to manifest His righteousness and holiness as the Lord of all nations. The Bible is His everlasting and eternal Word in which Elohim has declared that He alone is the

Creator of the universe. Therefore, He has the right to rule and reign as the Sovereign Lord over the heavens, the earth, and all of its inhabitants.

As a loving Father, God has sworn that He would never forsake the world that is suffering under demonic oppression, hatred, and violence. Through Jesus Christ, His Son, He offers His salvation to all of humanity. " For God so loved the world that He gave His only begotten Son, that whosoever believes in Him would not perish, but have everlasting life"(John 3:16). Spirit of Truth reveals "the righteousness of God through faith in Jesus Christ to all who believe for all have sinned and fallen short of the glory of God, being justified freely by His grace through the redemption that is in Christ Jesus" (Romans 3:21-24). In His creation, God has revealed His goodness, power, and presence. All His ways are perfect. The everlasting Father has spoken to His children in His own words assuring them that His plan of redemption through His Son Jesus Christ shall indeed be accomplished.

The Hebrew Alphabet –
Revelation of the Trinity

In His Own Words: Messianic Insights into the Hebrew Alphabet, L. Grant Luton illuminates the truth about the work of the Trinity revealed in the Creation story of Genesis. Through his study of the Hebrew alphabet, Luten has opened up a deeper revelation of the Trinity and their unique work of Creation and Redemption. The Father, the Son, and the Holy Spirit have lived from everlasting to everlasting in a timeless eternity. As a divine community, they designed and brought forth a magnificent cosmos with innumerable stars and galaxies. Today, astronomers continue to observe His vast universe over which He rules and reigns. The heavens and the earth are subject to His supreme authority and power. Moreover, God created humanity as spiritual beings with the capacity to experience an intimacy that exists between the Father, Son, and Holy Spirit. As social beings, they seek fellowship with God and one another. Through walking in obedience to the Word of God, His children fulfill His design and purpose for them in His original creation that is recounted through *His Own Words*. Every Hebrew word written in the account of Creation carries significant meaning for both Jews and Christians.

The first word in Genesis one is *B'reshite*. [2] The meaning of *B,reshite* is "In the beginning". The word that is pronounced *Barasheit* begins with the Hebrew letter *Bet*. In the beginning the Father, Son, and Holy Spirit had lived eternally as the Holy Trinity before the Creation. *Av*, the Father is the first letter of the Hebrew alphabet. *Bet,* the Son, is the second letter that stands to the right of *av*. Furthermore, the Hebrew word for son is *Ben*. Thus, the actual

---

[2] L.Grant Luton, *In His Words: Messianic Insights into the Hebrew Alphabet,* (Uniontown, Ohio: Beth Tikkun Publishing, 1999), 27.

meaning of the name Benjamin is Son of my Right Hand. This name reveals the exalted position of Jesus as the Son of God, who as *Bet* sits at the Right Hand of God the Father *Av*. (Matthew 26:64). The first two letters of the Hebrew alphabet reveal the perfect unity, harmony, and the intimate fellowship of Father and Son. He is the Word of God who has been with God the Father throughout all eternity. The Gospel of John reveals the unique relationship of the Father and His Son by alluding to Genesis 1:1. In His Gospel, John, the evangelist, boldly declares that Jesus is the eternal Word of God. "In the beginning was the Word, and the Word was with God, and the Word was God" (John 1:1). Jesus is *ho' logos*. [3] In the beginning before Creation, Yeshua, the Son, *Ben* was with His Father *Av*. The first two letters of the Hebrew alphabet reveal the eternal existence of the Father and His Son. *Aleph* and *Bet* stand next to one another in a perfect, harmonious partnership. While *Aleph* is a silent letter, *Bet* is a consonant letter that is pronounced as "B". The first letter of the Hebrew alphabet is vocalized as a breathy sound in the back of the throat. *Aleph* represents the Father as the silent One who speaks His Word through His Son. The Son as the Word of God speaks the Word that He has heard from His Father. "He who sent Me is true, and I speak to the world those things which I heard from Him" (John 8:26). The Word of the Father gives strength and power to the Son and to those who follow and obey Him. Moreover, Jesus had always obeyed His Father and remained faithful to Him throughout His earthly ministry. The Word of His Father sustained Him in all His trials and temptations. In the wilderness, Jesus faced His adversary, Satan and declared to him, "It is written, 'Man shall not live by bread alone, but by every word that proceeds from the mouth of God'" (Matthew 4:4). The Word of the Father is the bread that sustained His Son. Jesus, the Son of God, was strengthened through His obedience to the will of His Father. No one could persuade Him to turn away from His mission to redeem humanity at the cross.

---

[3] Ibid.

In His life and ministry, Jesus revealed that God the Father is the number One Person ruling over all creatures in heaven and on earth.

The first letter of the Hebrew alphabet, *Aleph* signifies the Father as the First Person of the Trinity. He is glorified through His Son. (John 17) He is the eternal One who rules over the Universe as the Sovereign Lord. *Bet* signifies Jesus, as the second Person of the Trinity, sent by His Father for the purpose of reconciling sinners. Through His substitutionary death, Jesus demonstrated the unfailing love of the Father for humanity. Through His voluntary death for the salvation of humanity, the Jesus showed the full extent of His love and devotion for His Father.

Jesus was sent by the Father to establish His Kingdom of righteousness, peace, and joy on earth. The Kingdom of God is the central message of Jesus' teachings (Matthew 13). In Matthew 6:9, Jesus taught His disciples to address God as Father in the Lord's Prayer. Through their redemption in Christ, the Son, His disciples have free access to God. Therefore, they call Him "Our Father." As His children, they echo the prayer of their Father and His Son declaring that His Kingdom and His will be accomplished on earth as it is in heaven. The prayer of the Son reveals the overall purpose and vision of God: "Father, You shall rule." The eternal rule of God who is the beginning and the end is declared throughout the Hebrew alphabet.

The fourth word in Genesis 1:1 is *et* that consists of the first and last letters of the Hebrew alphabet *Aleph* and *Tov*.[4] Yeshua (Jesus' name in Hebrew) is called the Word, the *Alpha* and *Omega*, the beginning and the end (Revelation 22:13-16). He was sent by God to bring reconciliation of men to Himself, establishing a new order. His mission on earth was to destroy the kingdom of Satan so that he would no longer have dominion over nature and men. Sin and death would be conquered through His death and resurrection. In His triumph over death, He was the first- fruits of those who have died. (I

---

[4] Ibid.

Kathleen Martinez

Corinthians 15:20) When Jesus came to earth to preach the Gospel of the Kingdom of God, He declared "The time is fulfilled and the Kingdom of God is at hand. Repent and believe the Gospel" (Mark 1:15). In the beginning of the Gospel of Mark, Jesus immediately went about the cities of Galilee performing great wonders, signs, and miracles. In His ministry, Jesus demonstrated the power and the presence of the Kingdom of God. His amazing works were performed so that the lost souls of men would be drawn to God. As a demonstration of the love and power of the Father, His works validated and proved the claim of the Spirit who declared in the opening title of the Gospel of Mark that Jesus is the Son of God. He gave the Son the power to do His works. The Holy Spirit descended upon Jesus at His baptism empowering Him to perform His works. "The Spirit of the Lord is upon Me, because He has anointed Me to preach good tidings to the poor; He has sent Me to heal the broken hearted, to proclaim liberty to the captives, and the opening of the prison to those who are bound; to proclaim the acceptable year of the Lord" (Isaiah 61:1, 2; Luke 4:18). When He cast out demons by the power of the Holy Spirit, Jesus was proclaiming that presence of the Kingdom of God was here on earth to destroy the works of the Devil (Matthew 12:28).

Through His death on the cross, Christ defeated death as the last enemy of humanity and put it under His feet (I Corinthians 15:26, 27). On the third day, Jesus arose as the victorious Ruler. And He will continue to reign until all things are under His feet. Upon His return, Jesus will rule over the nations so that the Kingdom of God will be fully established. Until His second coming, His followers are made to be more than conquerors in Christ, having no fear of Satan. Possessing eternal life, they are not subject to the power of death over them. In the end of this present world, on the Judgment Day, the Lord will cause the Devil and his angels to be cast into the Lake of Fire. Sadly, the lost whose names are not found in the book of life, will face the same terrifying judgment of Christ, the Righteous Judge who sits upon His throne. He will declare that their punishment is eternal death in the Lake of Fire (Revelation 20:10-15). Because Jesus Christ now rules over all principalities and powers, and rulers of darkness, and spiritual hosts of wickedness in the heavenly places, all Christians are able to withstand the evil day by taking on the whole Armor of God (Ephesians 6:10-13). They anticipate with great joy the day when the Jesus, the Son, returns the Kingdom of God to His Father.

In His joyous triumph, Jesus will present the Kingdom of God to the Father. Everything will be made new, for the first heaven and earth will have passed away. After God creates a new heaven and a new earth, the tabernacle of God will be with men and He will dwell with them forever as He did in the Garden of Eden before the Fall of Adam and Eve (Revelation 21). The book of Revelation discloses the ultimate vision of God who gives His saints hope of a bright future. The beauty of God's holiness and righteousness will be fully restored in His people. They will have free access to the Tree of Life that was once stood in the Garden of Eden. All old things associated with sin and death shall be removed from the presence of the Holy Father. He will not be reminded of the presence of sin. Furthermore, the complete restoration of paradise is the promise of God to all who remain loyal to Him in times of trials and tribulations. In his first letter, Peter declares that the saints of God possess a "living hope through the resurrection of Jesus Christ from the dead to an inheritance incorruptible and undefiled and that does not fade away reserved in heaven" (First Peter 1:1, 2). Facing severe persecution under Roman emperor Nero, the church in the first century was comforted by these words of Peter. As His faithful servants, their glorious inheritance in Christ awaited them in heaven. No man would be able to rob them of their salvation or steal their crown of everlasting life. In the Old Testament, the visions from God that came to Daniel revealed to the Jews in exile that He is the everlasting Sovereign over the nations.

In a night vision, Daniel saw the Ancient of Days sitting upon His throne. The Son of Man approached the Ancient of Days to give the Kingdom back to His Father. "One like the Son of Man came to the Ancient of Days. And they brought Him before Him. Then to Him was given dominion and glory and a kingdom that all peoples, nations, and languages should serve Him. His dominion is an everlasting dominion which shall not pass away And His Kingdom, the one which shall not be destroyed" (Daniel 7:13, 14). This night vision declares that the everlasting rule and dominion of God will not be overtaken by any power in heaven or on earth. How did the heavens and earth come into being? The first chapter of Genesis records the story of Creation. God created the heavens and the earth by the power of His Word.

The Creation of the Heavens and the Earth

In the beginning, God (Elohim) created the heavens and the earth. *Hashamayim we ha'erats* [5] Notice that the heavens is a plural noun whereas the earth is a singular noun. Both nouns have a definite article, and are linked together by a conjunction. The countless stars, planets, and galaxies are a part of His immense universe that modern scientists have recently been able to observe on earth through their telescopes. They are able to view the depth of the universe through colorful, detailed photographs from the Hubble Space telescope. "The heavens declare the glory of God and the firmament shows His handiwork" (Psalm 9:1-4). The Solar system is amongst a myriad stars in the Milky Way. Innumerable galaxies of His handiwork are being explored by astro-physicists who observe in their great amazement the glory of God. As a result, many scientists have come to the knowledge of their Creator and acknowledge His glorious, majestic existence. Moreover, the display of His magnificent universe is seen throughout the entire world, so that humanity is without excuse in their denial of their Creator *Elohim*. In Genesis one, the word for God *Elohim* is a uni-plural noun that implicates the Trinity. They brought everything into existence by the power of His spoken Word [6] (Hebrews 1:3). *Bara* a singular verb in Hebrew that means "bringing into existence something new, something that did not exist before" [7] Only Elohim is able to create new things: all matter, energy, space, and time out of nothing ex *nihilo*.

---

[5] Hugh Ross, *The Genesis Question: Scientific Advances and the Accuracy of Genesis* (Colorado Springs, Colorado: NavPress Publishing Group, 1998), 19-27.

[6] Ibid. 195.

[7] Ibid. 19, 59-61,62.

Kathleen Martinez

On Mount Sinai, God gave to Moses the biblical account of Creation (Exodus 19). Through His divine revelation of Creation, the events are accurately presented in their proper order: the physical universe, living plants and animals, and lastly, humanity as spiritual beings made in His image and likeness. In other Near Eastern cultures, other accounts of creation have been recorded. The *Enuma Elish,* an Akkadian story, was written during the reign of Hammurabi the Great around 1750 B.C. [8] It depicts a similar sequence of events: chaos on earth covered by water, the creation of Light, followed by the creation of land, the appearance of heavenly bodies for signs, seasons, and days, creation of land animals and creeping creatures. However, the Akkadian creation story is inaccurate in that it asserts that the heavenly bodies, land, and human beings were created from the corpses and blood of their gods who perished in combat. In the African account of creation, *Mbere,* the creator made human beings first and not last. Thus, the imaginations of men from other nations were not able to accurately construct the story of creation. In reality, only God Himself through His revelation to Moses could give an accurate and true account of how He created His Universe at a specific time in history. "I have declared the former things from the beginning. They went forth from My mouth, and I caused them to hear it. Suddenly, I did them, and they came to pass" (Isaiah 48:3). Through the prophet Isaiah, the Lord declared to Israel that He is the Creator, the First and the Last. "Listen to Me, O Jacob, and Israel, My called: I am He, I am the First, and I am also the Last. Indeed, My hand has laid the foundation of the earth. And My Right Hand has stretched out the heavens; When I call to them, they stand up together" (Isaiah 48:12, 13). Though the prophets of the Hebrew Bible, the Lord God asserts that He is the Creator who is the first and the last exercising His full authority over the heavens and the earth. Nothing came into existence before Him nor did Creation suddenly appear without Him. In the epistle to the Romans, Paul

---

[8] Ibid. 59-61.

addressed the false belief that a Creator does not exist. The Apostle Paul wrote that the wickedness of men suppress the knowledge of God as Creator of the world.

> The wrath of God is revealed from heaven against all ungodliness and unrighteousness of men who suppress the truth in unrighteousness because what may be known of God is manifest in them, for God has shown it to them. Since the creation of the world, His invisible attributes are clearly seen, being understood by the things that are made, even His eternal power and Godhead, so they are without excuse., because they knew God, they did not glorify him as God nor were thankful, but became futile in their thoughts and their foolish hearts were darkened.   Romans 1:18-21.

Kathleen Martinez

The Shifting of a Point of View from heaven to earth[9]

In Genesis 1:2, there is a dramatic shift in the frame of reference from outer space to the planet earth. According to Hugh Ross and other Christian astro-physicists, the biblical revelation accurately describes the chronological events of creation revealing the initial chaotic conditions on the face of the Earth. "Now the earth was formless and empty, darkness was over the surface of the deep, and the Spirit of God was hovering over the waters" (Genesis 1:2). The waters covered the whole surface of the earth. "You covered it with the deep as with a garment; the waters stood above the mountains" (Psalm 104). *Tohu wabohu* are Hebrew words that describe the earth as, "formless and empty." Since the 1990's, the astronomers have observed young stellar objects (YSOs) that are disks surrounded by a shell of gases of hydrogen, helium, methane, and ammonia, and dust debris.[10] All new planets are formed with opaque atmospheres. Moreover, the study of the earth's oldest rocks reveals that water like a blanket covered the entire earth. As cold and dark planets, Jupiter and Saturn still remain surrounded by a gas cloud of dust and debris.

---

[9] Ibid. 21-27
[10] Ibid., 26,27.

Light Appears on Earth

And God said, "Let there be Light" and there was light (Genesis 1:3). And Elohim issued a command saying, " Let there be" (Jussive imperative form of *haya* Strong's # 1961) *Haya* is a verb that means to cause to become; to cause to appear or arise; to cause to be made or done; come into existence; come to pass, make into something.[11] In the natural, light as the dominant form of energy, dispels the darkness at the time of creation and in this present age. On the surface of the earth's darkness, light breaks forth in all its magnificent brilliance and power. Elohim divided the light from the darkness. He called the light day and the darkness night. He saw that the light was good at the close of the first day that is a lengthy epoch of His creation. [12] The Hebrew word *Yom* is defined as sunrise to sunset; sunset to sunset; a space of time; an age; a time or period (without reference to solar days). Moreover, a day with the Lord is a thousand years (Psalm 90:4).

In the Gospel of John, the evangelist alluded to the light stating that Jesus is the Word of God. He is the Light that came into the world of darkness and chaos that had ruled over humanity for thousands of years.When the Son of God became flesh and dwelt among men, the glorious light of the Father's Presence became reality. (John 1:14) As the Light of the world, Jesus came to destroy the darkness. "He who sins is of the devil, for the devil sinned from the beginning. For this purpose the Son of God was manifested that He might destroy the works of the devil" (I John 3:8). The dark domain of Satan's kingdom would be conquered and overcome by Christ who is Light of the world. Now His people rejoice in the Light of His glory; they live a life of joyous victory.

---

[11] Ibid., 195.
[12] Ibid.,196,13.

Kathleen Martinez

The Second Day: Creation of the Atmosphere and the Water Cycle

On the second day of Creation, Elohim made an expanse or atmosphere that is immediately above the surface of the earth. *Raqia* is a Hebrew word that refers to an expanse, a visible dome of the sky. [13] He commanded the formation of an expanse or atmosphere that would separate the waters from the waters. To sustain life on earth, God created a water cycle of condensation and precipitation. Elohim called the expanse 'sky' (*Shamayim*) a visible dome of sky above and in which clouds move, the realm in which celestial bodies move, the spiritual realm in which God and the angels dwell and operate... The Hebrew writings referred to the three heavens (II Corinthians 12:1-4)[14] In his second epistle to the Corinthians, Paul recounted one of his visions in which he was caught up to the third heaven, and beheld the eternal throne room of God.

In the third heaven, the Father and the Son are enthroned; they are surrounded by angelic hosts who continually rejoice before them (Isaiah 6:1). Shouting for joy, they observed Father and Son create the physical universe (Job 38:7). In Proverbs eight, the writer under the guidance of the Spirit, described the collaboration of the Father and Son. When the heavens were being prepared, a master craftsman was "brought up" beside God. [15] The Wisdom of the Son of God was present with the Father. Throughout eternity, He was rejoicing always before Him. (Proverbs 8:27-28) He has always been the delight of God, the Father who expressed His love and approval of His Son at His public baptism. "This is my Beloved Son, in whom

---

[13] Ibid., 194.

[14] Ibid., 195.

[15] Jack Hayford, ed. *New Spirit-Filled Life Bible; Kingdom Equipping Through the Power of the Word.* (Nashville, Tennese: Thomas Nelson, Inc. 2002), 813.

I am well pleased" (Matthew 316, 17). Jesus, His beloved Son is revealed as the Word of God in John 1:1, 2. "In the beginning was the Word and the Word was with God and the Word was God." In John 11:25, Jesus declared that He is the Resurrection and the Life.

"When He prepared the heavens, I was there. When He drew a circle on the face of the deep, When He established the clouds above, When He strengthened the fountains of the deep, When He assigned to the sea its limit... Then I was beside Him as a master craftsman," (Proverbs 8:30). The Identity of the Wisdom of God was shrouded in mystery. Who was He? In the New Testament, the Wisdom of God is revealed as the second Person of the Trinity. The crucifixion of the Son of God revealed the Wisdom of God, " a mystery, the hidden wisdom which God ordained before the ages for our glory, which none of the rulers of this age knew; or had they known,they would not have crucified the Lord of glory" (I Corinthians 2:7,8).

The Formation of Land and
Seas on the Third Day

On the third day, Elohim gathered the waters into one place and assigned to them boundaries causing the ocean floor to arise and appear as dry land. In preparation for a biomass of diverse and complex life, He created an exact ratio of 29% land He called "Earth" and 71% of water surface known as "Seas". [16] Then God said, "Let the land produce vegetation, seed bearing plants (*Zera*) embryos of plants, trees and grasses and any plant species), and trees on the land that bear fruit with seed in it, according to their various kinds. And it was so." (Genesis 1:11) [17] When God spoke His creative Word, the earth brought forth a great abundance of lush vegetation providing a plant based diet that would nourish all animals and human beings. "And God saw that it was good" (verse 12). Today science recognizes that the providence of God is good; His food nourishes and preserves the life of all creatures. In contrast, man-made processed foods and GMO's (Genetically Modified Organisms) so prevalent in the American diet, is a major cause of disease and obesity. Moreover, many doctors are recognizing the importance of consuming a plant-based diet, for it is the best medicine that miraculously restores health and vitality to their patients. [18]

---

[16] Hugh Ross, *The Genesis Question: Scientific Advances and the Accuracy of Genesis* (Colorado Springs, Colorado, NavPress, 1998), 37-42.

[17] Ibid., 195.

[18] Suzanne Somers, *Knockout: Interviews with Doctors who are Curing Cancer and How to Prevent Getting it in the First Place* (New York, Harmony Books, 2009), 42.

The Appearance of the Sun, Moon and Stars in the Heavens on the Fourth Day

And God said, "Let there be lights in the expanse of the sky to separate the day from the night, and let them serve as signs to mark seasons and days and years."

Genesis 1:14

On the fourth day, God commanded lights in the sky to separate the day from the night. (Sign, *ot* ; Strongs #226.) The luminaries serve as a sign, signal, measuring mark, token, omen or evidence of His timing and purpose. [19] Heavenly bodies mark seasons, days, and years. (Season, *mo'ed* ; Strongs #4150.) A season is a fixed time, appointment, an appointed season, festival, feast, solemn assembly, and an appointed place for meeting. The first mention of *mo'ed* is found in Genesis 1:14[20] Stars, viewed for the first time on earth as luminaries, serve as signs or markers of times and seasons. Furthermore, light is a manifestation of God's omnipresence and power over darkness. His purpose in creating the universe was to bring glory to Himself (Psalm 19:1). In the last decade of the twentieth century, physicists have discovered that Elohim created matter and energy along with the space-time dimensions at specific moment in history. Their discovery supports the biblical claim that the universe had a definite beginning in finite time.[21] The Lord God has complete control of time and requires His people to make

[19] Hugh Ross, 196.
[20] Jack Hayford, Ed. *New Spirit-Filled Life Bible: Kingdom Equipping Through the Power of the Word.* (Nashville, Tennessee: Thomas Nelson, Inc. 2002), 187.
[21] Hugh Ross., 21.

Kathleen Martinez

wise use of their time on earth. Therefore, He admonishes them to number their days so that they may gain a heart of wisdom. Moreover, they gain wisdom by walking in the fear of the Lord who is the eternal and everlasting God. (Psalm 90:12). According to the writer of Ecclesiastes, "To everything there is a season, a time for every purpose under heaven." (Ecclesiastes 3:1). He has ordered the seasons to continue until the present heaven and earth pass away. At such time when He puts an end to all sin, rebellion, and wickedness, God will create a new heaven and a new earth (Revelation 21:1). All the former things that were marred by evil and corruption will be replaced with the new.

You Lord, in the beginning laid the foundation of the earth, and the heavens are the works of Your hands, they will perish but You remain. And they will grow old like a garment Like a cloak You will fold them up, and they will be changed. But You are the same and Your years will not fail. Hebrews 1:10-12

Creation of Lower Vertebrates and Soul Creatures on Day Five

> And God said, "Let the water teem with living creatures, and let birds fly above the earth across the expanse of the sky. So God created the great creatures of the sea. and every living and moving thing with which the water teems, according to their kinds, and every winged bird, according to its kind. And God saw that it was good. God blessed them and said, "Be fruitful and increase in number and fill the water. In the seas, and let the birds increase on the earth." Genesis 1:20-22.

After an immeasurable length of time of preparing earth for life, God commanded the water to become filled to overflowing with living creatures. Through the power of His creative word, He brought forth winged creatures souring above the earth, and great creatures teeming in the seas. He declared that all living things were good and blessed them. In the presence of the elements of light, water cycle, a protective atmosphere (ozone), and seasons marked by luminaries, the biomass was able to thrive on earth. God commanded the lower vertebrates and *nephesh* to be fruitful, grow in great abundance, and fill the earth. *Nephesh*, a Hebrew noun, denotes a creature that possesses a soul: person, mind, land creature with the breath of life, has capability to communicate emotions, desires, and will. The attributes of a soul are the mind, will, and emotions.[22] *Nephesh such as* birds and mammals were created to be at a higher level of existence capable of forming relationships with one another and with humanity. God created them to be friends and close companions who

---

[22] Hugh Ross., 49.

are able to show unconditional love to their masters. For thousands of years, mankind has developed strong emotional ties with domestic animals and regards them as children who need special attention and care. As family pets, animals are very sensitive to the emotions of people. Their senses are heightened to the sights and sounds that are generally unobserved by human beings. Moreover, they are trained to respond to emergencies such as accidents, injuries, and pain.

Creation of Specialized Land Animals and Man on Day Six

On the sixth day, God produced three specific kinds of land animals.[23] *Behema, remes, and chayya* are all soul creatures or nephesh. *Behema* and *chayya* are long-legged land animals such as horses, donkeys, and oxen that are utilized by mankind for agriculture and transportation. *Remes* are classified as short-legged land mammals such as rabbits, mice, cats, and dogs. Although they lived in a reciprocal relationship with human beings, the soul creatures do not have the capacity to enjoy a spiritual relationship with their Creator who generously provides daily for their physical needs. Therefore, God desired to bring forth an earthly family that would be an extension of His spiritual community in heaven. *Elohim* would design and form humanity that would resemble Him in His divine character and nature. As embodied creatures, they would be created as spiritual beings who would commune with their Creator. At the end of the sixth day, in the presence of His heavenly hosts, God formed humanity (Adam) a male and a female for His glory. God designed a man and his wife to generate for Himself a human family on earth through sexual intimacy. Set apart from all other creatures, a man and his wife would experience the rich and abundant blessings of their Creator who would place them in a pristine environment. As a lush garden of breathless beauty and majesty, the earth was a paradise brimming with vast numbers of living species. All men would grow in an intimate relationship with their Father in heaven and with one another. Furthermore, they would reflect the glory of Elohim: the Father, the Son and the Holy Spirit who live in a perfect community. All the heavenly hosts would marvel at the creation of Adam. Humanity would be God's magnificent masterpiece made in His image and likeness.

---

[23] Hugh Ross., 52, 53.

Humanity Created In His Image and Likeness

A dramatic portrait of a beautiful woman captures the attention of guests as they enter the spacious home of the Martinez family. Her quiet dignity commands the respect of many people who are drawn to her elegance, charm, and grace of character. Growing up in a distinctive home in San Francisco, Marjorie Moore was trained to be a lady who would represent the highest moral standards, values, and etiquette of her family. Living in the upper class of society with wealth and privilege, this young lady was cognizant of her identity, and possessed a clear sense of who she was. Her proud parents sent her to Mills Seminary, a well known prestigious institution for women. A liberal arts education furnished Marjorie with a deeper knowledge of a wide variety of disciplines, as well as valuable training in social skills. When Marjorie completed her education at Mills, she was well prepared to carry out her responsibilities as a confident lady, wife, and mother. At the tender age of nineteen, she met and married Hugh Brown, a well known lawyer who undertook a legal practice in a small western outpost far away from the Bay Area. On the night of their wedding, Mr. Brown and his stunning bride traveled by stagecoach to Tonopah, a small mining town in the desert of Nevada. In this rough and rugged arid environment, Mrs. Brown demonstrated resilience as she was willing to adapt to her new way of life. The young couple resided in a small three bedroom house where she raised their three children in the first decade of the twentieth century. Moreover, she had no servants to assist her at domestic duties. By the sweat of her brow, she accomplished her daily work of caring for her young children, entertaining frequent guests, cooking meals, washing clothes, and maintaining a clean house in a hot and dusty wilderness. During the closing days of the old western frontier, she managed to raise and discipline her two sons, Hugh and Marshall and a daughter Jerrie without the assistance of her husband who was overburdened with his legal practice. After sixteen years of living in a desert town, the Browns returned to San Francisco Bay Area, bought a large, elegant house in Palo Alto, and lived in prosperity for a short time. Due to a lingering illness, Mr. Brown continued his law practice for only about ten years. After a long battle with cancer, he passed away in the prime of his life. Many friends and family admired Mrs. Brown for her vibrant spirit and courage during a time of her bereavement. Due to her amazing inner strength, determination, and fortitude, she managed the Brown estate with wisdom. A strict upbringing enabled Mrs. Brown to maintain her positive disposition that contributed to her prosperity and longevity. Moreover, for many decades, she was diligently seeking God for further knowledge concerning spiritual reality.

For over sixty years, she studied the major religions of the world. Moreover, she faithfully attended the Unitarian Church that strictly opposes the doctrines of the Christian faith and, in particular, the deity of Christ. Throughout many years, she sensed a deep hunger in her spirit to know God, experience His love, wisdom and saving grace. . Many of her questions concerning salvation were left unanswered. How does one obtain an inner peace and serenity with God? What happens when a person dies? Does one enter into eternal life? Is there really a heaven and a hell? In the last decade of her life, the Spirit of the Lord was sensitive to her cry to encounter the Truth about God in the Bible. She was fascinated by the letters she had received from her granddaughter, who had recently become a born again Christian. As a young believer, she would often share her faith from various biblical passages on being born again. (John 3:16).

One afternoon, her granddaughter and fiancé came to visit her in her retirement home. When they offered to give her a tract about salvation, she refused it. However, after lunch, the young couple went to a piano to sing a love song. Hopefully, the song about God's

Kathleen Martinez

love would touch her heart. While she listened to their worship, Mrs. Brown sensed the overwhelming presence of the Lord. Through His love song, the Spirit of the Lord opened her heart to receive Jesus Christ as her personal Lord and Savior. At the advanced age of 95, she received the Lord Jesus as her Lord and Savior. The Gospel of Jesus Christ, the Living Word of God, quenched her thirst for a personal knowledge of the Truth. The image of God within her spirit that had been dormant for many years was quickened and came alive on the day she prayed for salvation. The angels of heaven rejoiced on the day she entered into the Kingdom of God. At the age of 103, she went into the glorious presence of God the Father. Throughout eternity, she will behold His glory in the company of all the angels and the redeemed.

In the Martinez house, many admire the beauty of her spirit that is captured in her portrait. This exquisite work of art was created in 1917 one hundred years ago. Today, it is a memorial of God's miraculous work of her salvation. Moreover, her portrait is a symbol of the work of the Holy Spirit who is restoring the image and likeness of God in the hearts and minds of His people. The greatest blessing of God is to be conformed to image of Jesus Christ, who came to earth as His Beloved Son to exhibit the loving nature of the heavenly Father, and to reflect the beauty of His holiness. Through the joyful testimony of Spirit- filled witnesses, the Kingdom of God is being published throughout all the nations. The lost see the radiance of the Lord in their daily lives. "How beautiful upon the mountains are the feet of him who brings good news, Who proclaims peace, Who brings glad tidings of good things, Who proclaims salvation, Who says to Zion, ' Your God reigns'" (Isaiah 52). In these last days, the Spirit of the Lord is being poured out upon all of humanity. "And it shall come to pass afterward that I will pour out My Spirit on all flesh" (Joel 2:28). Through the outpouring of the Holy Spirit, a great multitude from all nations is being drawn into His Kingdom. As a result, young people are experiencing an encounter with the Father of the Lord Jesus Christ. Through their dynamic worship of the Lord, their lives are being radically transformed into His image and likeness. Consequently, through the preaching of the Gospel of Jesus Christ, the Kingdom of God is rapidly advancing on earth in fulfillment of Genesis 1:26, 27.

In Genesis 1:26, 27, God proclaims His will and marvelous plan to create humanity in His image and likeness. What was His noble purpose of designing mankind? In reality, His vision has always been to extend His Kingdom over the entire face of the earth. What is the Kingdom of God? The Kingdom of God is His rule and dominion over His entire universe. As the one and only Creator of all things, Elohim has the divine right, power, and authority to govern His Creation as His domain according to His perfect will. Moreover, His Kingdom is without end, for it is established with judgment and justice. (Isaiah 9:7) The ruler-ship of God is characterized by His righteousness, peace, and joy. (Romans 14:17) His throne is established upon truth and righteousness "Your throne, O God is forever and ever; A scepter of righteousness is the scepter of Your Kingdom" (Psalm 45:6). Righteousness that characterizes His government conforms to His moral laws that cannot be broken. Nor can they be altered by the laws of human government or false religions with their erroneous philosophies, vain imaginations or teachings. In America, the satanic lies and deception that opposes the truth of God's Word is now being exposed, confronted, and defeated by the bold Christian leadership of God's people. The believers in the Kingdom of God will no longer tolerate the lies that have been taught by leftists and liberals who have come out of many educational institutions in the last several decades. It is time to stand up and contend for the Christian and Judaic faith upon which America was founded. In his epistle, Jude declared, "I found it necessary to write to you exhorting you to contend earnestly for the faith which was once for all delivered to the saints" (Jude 3). Many scientists through diligent research and observation have come to a personal knowledge of God. The Truth of His laws and sovereign rule over the heavens that contain a myriad number of galaxies are being observed by physicists who by faith now embrace the reality of His glorious presence. His Truth that is openly proclaimed in the physical universe will always challenge the disbelief in the hearts of men. "The heavens declare the glory of God And the firmament shows His handiwork" (Psalm 19:1). Facing the daily unrelenting satanic attacks of secularism in American society, will the upright remain faithful to Him at all times?

Consider the testing of Job, who cried out to God in his trials and tribulation. What was the cause of his intense pain and suffering? In the book of Job, Satan had approached God and questioned the faithfulness of Job. As the accuser, Satan hates God and humanity who is made in His divine image and likeness. Humanity reflects the glory and majesty of the Creator. Would Job, who is blameless and upright in all his ways, remain faithful, fear God, and reject evil while facing the pressure of severe trials? Would Job question God's integrity and goodness while undergoing an overwhelming loss of his personal wealth, the death of his children, and the cynical remarks of rebellious wife? Moreover, would Job follow her advice, and curse God as excruciating boils covered his entire body? Moreover, how would he face the rejection of his wife, servants, and friends who denied him any comfort and emotional support? In his distress, Job desperately searched for truthful answers that his family and friends failed to offer him. In the end, he appealed to his Redeemer declaring" I know that My Redeemer lives!" (Job 19:25). After a long intercourse with his "friends", Job welcomed an encounter with the Almighty. In the midst of his trials and tribulation, God confronted Job with rhetorical questions. "Where were you when I laid the foundations of the earth?" (Job 38:4) "Moreover, the Lord answered Job, and said," Shall the one who contends with the Almighty correct Him? He who rebukes God, let him answer it" (Job 40: 2) Here, the Lord states that Job was in no position to question His Will and the sovereignty rule of his Creator. Moreover, the wisdom of God did not require his counsel or advice. In response, Job humbly responds, " I have heard of you by the hearing of the ear, But now my eye sees You" (Job 42: 5). By faith, humanity learns to trust in God, acknowledge His integrity in all His actions, and recognize that He is at work to complete His redemptive plan. Faith is the recognition that God knows all things from the beginning to the end. At the end of human history, His full redemption and restoration of humanity shall be accomplished. Therefore, He deserves the praise and adoration of His saints at all times. Who is Elohim? How does He present Himself in Genesis?

On the sixth day of creation, Elohim reveals Himself for the first time as "a community of persons" [24] Throughout eternity, three divine Persons work as relational Beings in perfect peace, harmony, and unity. How do they maintain their bond of unity? The Spirit of love is the bond of their perfection (Colossians 3:14). No satanic opposition to their Kingdom has the power to break their bond of love and unity. The organic structure of their unity will never be destroyed by the assault of enemy forces. The love of God is far greater in power than the hatred and hostility of men. Moreover, the throne of God has withstood the rebellion of Satan and his fallen angels. The divine love and faithfulness that bind the Father, Son and Holy Spirit is everlasting.

Consider how the relationship between the Father and His Son was tested at the opening of His ministry on earth. At the baptism of Jesus, the voice of the Father came from heaven, saying "This is my Beloved Son, in whom I am well pleased" (Matthew 3:17). Having made this public statement concerning His Son, the Father tested their relationship. In Matthew 4:1, "Jesus was led by the Spirit into the wilderness to be tempted by the devil." Would Jesus exercise His divine power to serve His own personal needs, to gain recognition by the religious authorities, or to establish His rule over the nations of the world without paying the ultimate price on the cross for

---

[24] 24 Larry Crabb, *Fully Alive: A Biblical Vision of Gender that Frees Men and Women to Live Beyond Stereotypes.* (Grand Rapids, Michigan : Baker Books, 2013), 34.

Kathleen Martinez

the salvation of humanity? In the wilderness, Jesus triumphed over Satan and remained faithful to the redemptive plan of His Father. Through the cross, He revealed the full extent of His Father's love for humanity. Therefore, all the redeemed of the Lord will forever praise the Lamb of God for their deliverance from sin and death.

The bond of love and intimacy uniting the Father and the Son and the Holy Spirit is beyond human understanding. Because the human heart is tainted with sin, no man is able to love God and others unselfishly. Therefore, the Spirit of love that binds the Father and the Son is here on earth. The capacity to love "has been poured out in our hearts by the Holy Spirit who was given to us" (Romans 5:5). The Spirit of God has imparted to his saints His power to love others as He loves them. According to Paul in his epistle to the Colossians, the followers of Christ are to "put on love which is the bond of perfection" (Colossians 3:14). How do the children of God enter into the perfect dance of divine love? Through experiencing the love of their heavenly Father in a personal relationship, they learn how to love each other as He loves them.

Consider John the Beloved who leaned on the breast of the Lord at the Last Supper, listening to the pulse of loving Heart of the Son and His Father. What is the essential message of the Gospel of John? The essential message of John is entering into the relational love of God through faith in Jesus Christ, the Son of God who is eternal life. "But these are written that you may believe that Jesus is the Christ, the Son of God, and that believing you may have life in His Name" (John 20:31).

Of all His disciples, the apostle known as the John the Beloved remained faithful to Jesus up to the day of His crucifixion. John was the only disciple who was supportive of Jesus at the time of His crucifixion. (John 19:25-27) John stood at the foot of His cross with Mary. Before His death, Jesus commended and entrusted the care of His mother into his loving hands. Through his intimate relationship with Jesus and Mary, His mother, John exemplified the relational love of God to the Body of Christ. I John 4:7, 8, the apostle John issued a command, "Beloved, let us love one another for love is of God; and everyone who loves is born of God and knows God. He who does not love does not know God for God is love." Through a personal relationship with Jesus, John and the other disciples experienced the unconditional love of the Father. During His earthly ministry, Jesus taught His disciples to love one another. The love of Christ was demonstrated by His humble and compassionate service toward all men. While He was carrying the burdens of others, Jesus committed Himself to the care of His Father. As He maintained His devotion to His Father, Jesus learned obedience through suffering. In this dark world, Jesus experienced being rejected by His friends, family, and the religious authorities. Moreover, He lived in poverty, under the political oppression of Roman rule and endured the relentless opposition of Satan.

On the eve of His crucifixion, Jesus gave His disciples a new commandment. "A new commandment I give to you that you love one another as I have loved you, that you love one another. By this all will know that you are my disciples, if you have love for one another" (John 13:34, 35). As the disciples obeyed His new commandment to love one another as He loved them, His divine image would be revealed to humanity. Through their love and unity, the Kingdom of God would be observed by all nations. In Genesis1:26, 27, God created man in His own image in order to extend His community of love and fellowship on earth.

Then God said, "Let us make man in Our image, according to our likeness" Genesis 1:26.

God declared His will in a "plural deliberation with Oneself" [25] The divine council consists of two or more Persons who expressed their desire to bring forth children who would reflect their relational existence of love and unity. "Let us make man" is the declaration of

---

[25] 25 Paul Jouon, S.J. and T. Muraoka, *A Grammar of Biblical Hebrew Volume ll Part Three: Syntax Paradigms and Indices.*(Roma: Editrice Pontificio Istituto Biblico,2000), 375.

God in the first person plural cohortative. The Divine Counsel is mirrored in a relationship between a man and a woman who love one another. Through their love and union, they will bring forth children created by God. On the night of their wedding, their marital love will be consummated in the intimacy of their sexual union. Their sexuality is sacred gift from God, for it reflects the love and the unity of the Father, the Son, and the Holy Spirit. Therefore, the sexual union under the canopy of marriage is the vehicle that the Creator has designed for the procreation of humanity on earth. Furthermore, what is man that God would be mindful of him?

Man was made a little lower than Elohim. (Psalm 8:5). What does it mean to be made in image and likeness of Elohim? According to Luton, humanity is made in *Tzelem* (Hebrew for Image) or in essence like Himself.[26] Man (*Adam*) is like Elohim: Father, Son, and Holy Spirit in personality, power, wisdom, love, and character. As a reflection of His Creator, man is created as a triune being with a body, soul, and spirit. The Soul (mind, will, and emotions) of the Father is expressed through His Word, the Son, and the Holy Spirit. The Word became flesh and dwelt among men for the purpose of revealing the glory of God (John 1:14). God prepared a body for His Son who came to earth to do His will, offering Himself up as a sacrifice for sin (Hebrews 10: 5-7). The Holy Spirit, of the Lord (*ruah Adonai*) descended upon Jesus at the time of His water baptism. The Lord anointed Him for His public ministry: to preach good news to the poor, to bind up the broken hearted, to proclaim freedom for the captives, and to release from darkness the prisoners, and to proclaim the year of God's favor. (Isaiah 61:1) Moreover, the same spirit who raised Christ from the dead, imparts His Spirit of life into humanity as spiritual beings. Immediately, at the very moment of their conception in the womb, all persons received the spirit of life from their Creator, for they are created as spiritual beings made in

---

[26] L. Grant Luton, *In His Own Words: Messianic Insights Into the Hebrew Alphabet.* (Uniontown, Ohio: Bethtikkun, 1999), 12-15.

the image of God. At the time of death, the same spirit is loosed, removed, and returned to God who gave it. "Remember you Creator before the silver cord is loosed, Or the golden bowl is broken, Or the pitcher shattered at the fountain, Or the wheel broken at the well. Then the dust will return to the earth as it was, and the spirit will return to God who gave it" (Ecclesiastes 12:6, 7). Every human being as a spiritual being is created to glorify God in their spirit, soul and body.

Moreover, the life of a child in the womb responds to life of the Spirit. Consider the response of John the Baptist leaping with joy in the womb of his mother when he heard the greeting of Mary to Elizabeth. Moreover, Elizabeth was filled with the Holy Spirit and declared to her cousin Mary, "Blessed are you among women and blessed is the fruit of your womb" (Luke 1:41, 42). Motherhood is a special blessing from God. The unborn child is the fruit of her womb that should never be destroyed by society nor viewed as an inconvenience.

Therefore, remember that all human beings are spiritual and social creatures who have the capacity to commune and have intimate fellowship with their Creator. For eternity, Elohim has been an intrinsic community of Persons enjoying warm and loving support of one another. Each Person of the Trinity has His unique Personality. Every human being is unique in personality, possessing a mind to think, a will to make decisions, and an emotional nature to express feelings. Through the five senses of the body, one interacts with the environment and with others. Just as there are natural senses of the body, there are spiritual ones. By faith, one can see, hear, discern, commune, and touch the Spirit of God in the spiritual realm. "No eye has seen, no ear has heard, nor has it entered into the heart of man the things which God has prepared for those who love Him. But God has revealed them to us by His Spirit" (I Corinthians 2:9-10).

In the presence of the heavenly hosts, Elohim did an amazing work when He created man as male and female. "So God created man in His own image; in the image of God He created him; male and female He created them. Then God blessed them. 'Be fruitful, and multiply; fill the earth and subdue it'" (Genesis 1:27, 28). What was the purpose of God creating gendered man as male and female? The desire of their Creator was to design the physical, emotional, and spiritual being of a male and a female to have the capacity to produce children in a loving and safe home environment established by Him within the sacred bond of marriage. Human sexuality as a sacred act was designed to be expressed solely under the canopy of a marriage covenant that must not be broken. Through the blessings of Elohim, mankind participates in the process of creating life. By the way, only God can create life! Through the miracle of procreation, humanity was made to be fruitful, multiply, fill the earth, and subdue it. What did God have in mind when He created man as gendered beings?

The Glory of God is Man Fully Alive

In American society, people often define gender in their own terms. A man is masculine because he is strong, handsome, and successful in the market place where he has accumulated great wealth, power, and influence. On the other hand, a woman is admired for her physical beauty, her various gifts and talents, and her accomplishments and influence both in the home and in the market place. However, in the eyes of God, masculinity and femininity are defined by His divine will and purpose In the creative Mind of God, a male and a female are relational beings who know how to treat others with love, respect, and compassion. Moreover, they obey His golden rule of treating others in the same manner that they wish to be treated, placing the needs of others first. Sadly, this is often not the case in American society. The desire of fallen humanity to gain wealth and recognition is caused by greed and ambition, bringing great harm to the earth and all of its inhabitants. Unfortunately, in the pharmaceutical and agricultural industries, the accumulation of great wealth overshadows the health and well-being of the public. Unfortunately, the over prescription of drugs lines the pockets of doctors who bow down under the control of the pharmaceutical companies. Therefore, the medical profession has become more and more corrupt and less trustworthy. Many patients are unaware of the dangerous side-effects of drugs and antibiotics that are often overprescribed by doctors. Furthermore, American industries pollute the air, water, and soil. The environment is full of toxins a major cause of all diseases such as cancer, heart failure, diabetes, arthritis, and dementia.

Unfortunately, the poor, sick, and needy are often ignored by many believers who are driven by their own interests and desire to achieve material success. The Spirit of God is grieved by their lack of sensitivity to the needs of others, for He has poured out His love and compassion in their hearts to care for the less fortunate. In His parable, Jesus taught His disciples to be a Good Samaritan in Luke 10: 25-37. The Good Samaritan saw a man who was stripped of his clothing, wounded and left half dead on the highway. Rather than passing him by, he showed compassion bandaging his wounds, pouring out the healing elements of oil and wine, transporting him to an inn and taking his time and expense to care for him. In the same manner, true servants of God, respond to the promptings of the Holy Spirit showing mercy to their neighbor. Today, Christian parents are to be proper models for their children showing of mercy to the misfortunate.

Under the guidance of the Holy Spirit, a young boy grows up spiritually to become masculine man. As a *zakar, he is* a mature man who is created " to leave a mark, to make an impact"[27] A man who remembers what is important in God's eyes, is motivated to do great things in the Kingdom of God. He is touched by the feelings and burdens of others and takes time to listen to the inner cry of their hearts. In other words, he is moved by compassion and exhibits the love and tender mercies of God. Likewise, God creates a young girl to become a feminine woman. As a *(neqebah)*, she is created to be one who is "punctured, bored through".[28] She is designed by God to invite (others into an intimate relationship with their Creator). She neither demands her way nor control others, but allows the Holy Spirit to convict them. Through her loving spirit, she is able to relate to people who are being challenged and overwhelmed by insurmountable hardships. Rather than demanding her own way and control others, a wise woman allows the Holy Spirit to convict them. Through her loving spirit, she is able to relate to people who are being challenged and overwhelmed by insurmountable hardships. Instead of becoming angry and resentful toward the discourtesy of others,

---

[27] Larry Crabb, *Fully Alive: A Biblical Vision that Frees Men and Women to Live Beyond Stereotypes.*(Grand Rapides, Michigan: BakerBooks, 2013), 66-68.
[28] Ibid., 43,44,45,46

she is able to extend her love and support to alleviate their pain. Moreover, through earnest prayer, she graciously places them into the Hands of God, trusting in Him to transform them. As a child of God, a feminine woman recognizes that she is totally dependent upon her heavenly Father to supply all her needs. "The Lord is my Shepherd. I shall not want." (Psalm 23:1) Her Creator is her Husband. "For your Maker is your husband, The Lord of hosts is His Name. And your Redeemer is the Holy One of Israel; He is called the God of the whole earth" (Isaiah 54:5). As a godly woman, she is "open to receive only what reflects God's character and advances His purposes". Her "relational femininity" is a reflection of the loving nature of God. Her lifestyle is characterized by an "openness to receive and willingness to give" unselfishly. Just as she opens up her heart to her heavenly husband to pour out His life to those around her, she opens up her body to her husband in order to conceive and bear children.

Moreover, in a marital relationship, both man and woman are in mutual submission to the Holy Spirit (Ephesians 5:24). Submission means to "arrange yourself under a larger design" [29] A wife adapts herself to her husband's plans and purpose. As an act of devotion to him, she is willing to sacrifice and lay aside her own will and personal desires to be his support. Her love enables him to accomplish his work and realize his dreams. Often, a wife must be patient while her husband completes his education before he is able to enter his field of work. Moreover, imagine a husband who enters into a lengthy military career that requires years of great sacrifice for the wife and their children. While a man is deployed for many months in a foreign land facing danger, the wife and children remain brave and pray for his safe return.

In the life of Christian men and women, the will of God is sought through daily devotion, service, and sacrifice so that His redemptive plan and purpose is accomplished. Through their living

---

[29] Ibid., 60.

Kathleen Martinez

testimony, His saints manifest the nature of His love and divine character of holiness. As they are ruled by the gentle Spirit of God, He convicts the hearts of sinners. The Spirit of the Lord is kind and patient. In dealing with humanity, the Spirit of the Lord never condemns nor does He break down the spirit of a man or a woman. He offers His loving counsel, support, and power that enable them to overcome sin and grow in godly character. Why does He emphasize the importance of character in His Kingdom? The effective ministry of God flows out of good Christian character. As mentioned earlier, Christians are created to reflect God's divine character. Consider how the daily actions of Christians in the market place and home, speak louder than words. When the righteousness of God is revealed in the conduct of His saints, the Kingdom of God is seen as a light in a dark world. The lost are drawn to the light when the truth of His love and compassion are revealed. The Kingdom of God is advanced when love wins over hate and peace overcomes violence.

"The Kingdom of Heaven suffers violence and the violent take it by force" (Matthew 11:12). When Jesus entered into this world, the hateful and destructive nature of the kingdom of Satan was exposed. His evil work was visibly shaken when the Lord cast out demons. While Christ conducted His ministry on earth, two kingdoms were visibly at war: the Kingdom of God and the kingdom of Satan. While religious leaders observed His signs, miracles, and wonders, they could not deny works of Christ. Due to their hardness of heart and unbelief, they accused Jesus of operating under the influence of Satan when He cast out demons. In response to them, Jesus answered them saying, "If Satan casts out Satan, he is divided against himself. How then will his kingdom stand?"...But if I cast out demons by the Spirit of God, surely the Kingdom of God has come upon you. Or how can one enter a strong man's house and plunder his goods, unless he first binds the strong man? And then he will plunder his house" (Matthew 12:26, 28, 29).

Christ, who demonstrated His power to plunder Satan's kingdom, is the perfect model for the church. God gave His saints the power and authority to conquer Satan and destroy his demonic domain. Both male and female, were made to be stewards over of all the creatures of earth. Furthermore, Adam was commanded to subdue, conquer, and defeat the kingdom of Satan.

> Let us make Adam in Our Image, according to Our likeness; let them have dominion over the fish of the sea, over the birds of the air, and over the cattle, over all the earth and over every creeping thing that creeps on the earth. So God blessed then, and God said to them, "Be fruitful, multiply; fill the earth and subdue it have dominion over the fish of the sea, over the birds of the air and over every living thing that moves on the earth. Genesis 1:27.

How successful is the church in her role of stewardship and the conquest of the forces of evil today? In American society, there are strong resentments and animosity of the liberals toward conservative point of view. An intensive cultural war between conservatives and progressives has been brewing for many decades, causing a sharp division among Americans. Liberals are attacking the Constitutional rights of American citizens to "life, liberty, and the pursuit of happiness". The traditional Judeo-Christian moral and ethical values are viewed by American society as "politically incorrect". Sadly, the sanctity of life has given away to a culture of death that declares that a woman has unrestrictive right over her body. However, the question by conservatives is now being raised. What about the right to life of the unborn child? For decades, the abortion industry has spread the lie that a woman has the right to choose her path in life rejecting the burdens of motherhood.

Although the act of abortion is a violent destruction of the valuable life of an unborn child, it is considered legal in the sight of men. However, in the eyes of the Creator of life, it is murder. Apparently, the convenience of the mother now overrules the right to life of the baby in her womb. Fortunately, the voice that supports the right of the unborn is being heard in America. Through the diligent prayers, and financial support of Christians, young women are being informed by pro-life organizations about the issues concerning abortion. How safe is abortion? What emotional and physical effects does undergoing abortion have on women? Students for Life an organization led by Kristen Hawkins is impacting the millennial generation with the truth. On high school and college campuses, an overwhelming majority of the young people is waking up to the reality that a significant number in their generation has been murdered by the abortion industry. Therefore, many young women of the millennial generation are defending the right to life of the unborn child. Moreover, in the election of 2016, Evangelical Christians responded to call of God through the ministry of Franklin Graham to vote and elect a prolife President, Congress, and Senate. More and more centers of abortion such as Planned Parenthood are being shut down while pregnancy resource centers are becoming more available for the care of women and their unborn children. When a woman discovers that she is pregnant, she feels alone, overwhelmed by the responsibilities of motherhood, and unable to financially support her child. However, when counselors are available to offer their guidance and support, many mothers do not seek an abortion. They realize that others are willing to assist them spiritually and financially.

Another intense battle in America is being waged for the sanctity of marriage. The divine institution of marriage between a man and a woman is being rejected and replaced by alternative lifestyles that are abominations in the sight of God. Unfortunately, fornication is no longer viewed as a sin. Living together may appear to be a rational decision and is considered a normal test of the relationship. If the relationship proves to be undesirable, there is no marital commitment to remain together nor is there an obligation to work through conflicts and disagreements. The love relationship is destroyed because of selfishness and pride that causes the main focus to be centered more on oneself than upon the needs and interests of others.

Today, more and more couples are living together as domestic partners. Why do they need a marriage license when they love one another? Gay marriage has become more and more acceptable as a civil union protected by law. Anyone who opposes gay marriage is ostracized and viewed as a hateful homophobe. However, courageous men and women of God have stood up for their faith and oppose spiritual darkness in American society. God is on the move!

In the Christian community lead by strong spiritual leaders, a new awakening is growing steadily as a strong political force. "When the enemy comes in like a flood, the Spirit of God will lift up a standard against him". (Isaiah 59:19). The preaching of the Word of God is convicting men and women of their sin of apathy, compromise, and self-centered lifestyle. The American believers as His people, are beginning to wake up to the call of God to humble themselves, pray, seek His Face, and turn from their wicked ways so that He may forgive their sin and heal their nation. (II Chronicles 7:14) Now, the lies and the "fake news" of the liberal media are being exposed for their attempts to remove Christians from their public office. Moreover, the arrogance of intellectual elites who in American universities boldly reject the Judeo-Christian faith is being exposed and challenged by Christian students. They are not ashamed of the Gospel of Christ "for it is the power of God to salvation for everyone who believes" (Romans 1:16). Having the Mind of Christ, they are well equipped to tear down vain philosophies of men and overcome any hostile intellectual environment with the Sword of God's Word. "And take the helmet of salvation and the sword of the Spirit which is the Word of God." (Ephesians 6:17)

Furthermore, the evangelical church will not surrender their traditional American civil rights and liberties to liberal courts and legislatures. The original intent of the framers of the Constitution of the United States will be upheld by God fearing Supreme Court Justices who will not legislate from the bench. Conservatives will

Kathleen Martinez

be vehement in their opposition to any legislation of the federal government or court decisions that would remove their right to freedom of speech, freedom to assemble, freedom of the press and more importantly, the freedom to express their faith. The Christian leadership of the American Center for Law and Justice under Jay Sekulow is taking legal action to defend life, liberty and the pursuit of happiness. Through prayer and financial support of the ACLJ, the Billy Graham Evangelical Association, Students for Life, the Christian Broadcasting Network, and other Christian organizations, a new awakening is restoring Judeo-Christian foundation that makes America a great nation. In 2016, signs of a New Awakening became evident as Evangelicals heard the call of God to go to the polls and elect Donald Trump for President. Our president supports the State of Israel and recognizes the horrific genocide of Christians by radical ISIS in the Middle East. In obedience to the Spirit of God, the church in America must exercise the power and authority of God taking dominion over wicked men and women who stir up hate and violence, disrupting the peace and unity in local communities. The Kingdom of God characterized by righteousness, peace and joy shall prevail through men and women who hear and obey the call of God to bear their responsibility of leadership. Through the redemptive work of the cross of Jesus Christ, the dignity and dominion of Humanity (*Adam*) has been restored. The work of the Spirit of God is to complete the restoration of Humanity as co-rulers with the Creator Elohim. The second chapter of Genesis, the book of beginning, reveals the creation of Adam in the Garden of Eden.

Living In The Presence of The Lord— Paradise of Genesis Two

In the 1950's and 1960's, Lake Oswego, a suburb of Portland, Oregon was a peaceful small town in which to raise a family. During this time, many young couples heard about the bustling housing market in the suburbs. They were attracted to the serenity and quietness of a densely wooded community surrounding a pristine blue lake. A healthy postwar economy produced a boom in the housing market. In June of 1950, a house for sale caught the attention of Duke Brown, a successful insurance executive, who had recently moved from the Bay Area up to Portland, Oregon located in the Northwest. As the younger son of Hugh and Marjorie Brown, he grew up in the desert town of Tonopah, Nevada. In 1920, his family moved to the city of Palo Alto, California where they purchased an impressive upper class residence. In the back of his mind, Mr. Brown held fond memories of his childhood home. One day, he saw an advertisement of a house for sale in Lake Oswego. Immediately, upon viewing it, he fell in love with the beauty of this house located in a dense forest of tall fir trees. Without considering the limits of his annual income, he did not hesitate to put a down payment of $2,000. The purchase of his dream house costing $20,000 would stretch the family budget. Why did he wish to own this particular Spanish-Tudor house in an upper middle- class neighborhood? Built in the year of 1930, the twenty year old residence closely resembled his childhood home in Palo Alto. Moreover, the two story house was about two miles away from downtown Lake Oswego and fifteen miles southwest of Portland. How would his precious wife respond to the new house? He assumed that she would fall in love with it. But when she walked into a dark kitchen and saw only a thin ray of light shining from a small window, she shook her head in protest saying, "No way!"

Kathleen Martinez

Quickly, her husband came up with a renovation plan and made a promise to remodel the kitchen. First, the dense forest of fir trees standing behind the house, blocking the sunlight would be cut down. Second, an enlarged window would be installed, producing a bright and cheerful atmosphere in the kitchen.

In Lake Oswego, Oregon, the American traditional way of life was like a paradise. The father, as the head of his household, provided a safe and secure home for His wife and children. During the 1950's, families left their homes unlocked having no fear of crime. The physical and emotional home environment was stable, wholesome, and ideal. Children were free to go outside to play with their neighbors. Parents enjoyed playing golf and puttering around in their gardens. What a fond dream about an idealistic childhood! Would it be possible to enjoy living in a paradise without crime and violence?

Does such a local community of love, unity, and friendship actually exist in America and in other nations of the world? In the hearts of devout men and women who are led by the Spirit of God in their daily lives, the divine love of God is present here and now. They have a "living hope through the resurrection of Jesus Christ from the dead to an inheritance... reserved in heaven" (I Peter 1:3, 4). In Christ, who arose from the dead, they anticipate a bright future in His Presence. Moreover, He lives and rules as their Lord and Savior. Therefore, joy is seen on their faces, having a freedom of spirit and peace of mind. At the dawn of human history, the first family enjoyed a care free existence, living in a paradise under the protection and provision of their heavenly Father. At the end of the sixth day of creation, God surveyed His creative work with great joy and satisfaction, declaring that all His work was very good. Moreover, the heavenly host marveled at the creation of His finest masterpiece Adam, a spiritual embodied soul, who reflected the glory and the majesty of God Himself.

Sanctification of the Seventh Day as the Day of Rest

Thus, the heavens and the earth, and all the host of them were finished.

> And on the seventh day, God ended His work which He had done, and He rested on the seventh day from all His work which He had done. Then God blessed the seventh day, and sanctified it, because in it He rested from all His work which God had created and made. Genesis 2:1-3

In the second chapter of Genesis on the seventh day, Elohim finished His initial creative work. The heavens, the earth, and all living things that He had spoken into being shouted His praises! On the seventh day, God literally ceased His work and rested. Thus, He instituted the Sabbath as a day of rest for humanity who would worship Him in celebration of His greatness and goodness. (*Shabbat* Strong's # 7673, a Hebrew verb meaning to cease, desist, or rest). Moreover, He blessed the seventh day, setting it apart as a sacred time, a period of twenty- four hours for rest, worship in grateful contemplation of his greatness, and recreation.

Through His mandate, unique places, times, seasons, and people were designated as sacred and holy. They were set apart for His service. The Lord God established appointments with His people for He longed to be with them in their daily lives in close intimate fellowship. Therefore, in the wilderness, Moses received a blueprint from heaven for a Tabernacle, a sacred tent of meeting in which the Lord God of Israel dwelt in the midst of the camp (Exodus 26). Surrounded by a courtyard marked of by a boundary of embroidered curtains, the sacred tent was designed to be a portable tabernacle that could easily be dismantled and carried by the Levites. Along with the priesthood, the Levites were set apart and appointed by the Lord God to administer animal sacrifices. The blood of these sacred offerings was presented before the Lord at the entrance of the Tabernacle to cover the sin of the people and cleanse away their personal defilement or impurity. Upon the completion of the Tabernacle, it was hallowed and made holy. "And you shall take the anointing oil, and anoint the tabernacle and all that is in it and you shall hallow it and all utensils and it shall be holy" (Exodus 40:9). (*Kodesh* Strong's #6944 is a Hebrew adjective that denotes apartness, sacredness).

In essence, the tabernacle of Moses was a reflection of the Garden of Eden as the first meeting place on earth between the Lord God and humanity. God had created Adam on the sixth day, the eve of the seventh day. Made in the flawless and perfect image and likeness of Elohim, God commanded Adam to rest from six days of labor, enjoying an intimate relationship with his heavenly Father. Before the Fall of Adam, harmony and peace characterized a perfect relationship between God and humanity who lived in a state of purity and innocence. In the evening, after Adam worked a full day, God would come down into the garden to speak to him face to face. In His Presence, he would find daily refreshment and renewal in his spirit, soul, and body. The twenty-third psalm depicts the paradise of the Garden of Eden as a pastoral scene of the Lord as the Great Shepherd caring for His sheep. "The Lord is my Shepherd; I shall not want. He makes me lie down in green pastures. He leads me beside the still waters. He restores my soul" (Psalm 23:1, 2). Under the care of their Shepherd, nothing is lacking for His people as He provides for all their basic necessities of life. In green pastures, the Lord causes them to lie down in a state of repose. (*rabaz* Strong's # 7257 a Hebrew verb meaning to stretch oneself out, lie down.) The Lord Jesus offers His rest to those who come to Him, overburdened with their own labor, having exhausted their own resources, discovering that they are unable to live up to His divine standards of righteousness. When they are overwhelmed by their own imperfections and failures, the Lord Jesus invites them to come to Him for encouragement, instruction and guidance. In exchange, they take up His yoke and learn His ways of gentleness and humility of heart. The soul finds relief no longer striving to obtain recognition and status through dead works. In the Kingdom of God, one finds rest putting one's trust in Jesus Christ who accomplished His complete work of salvation at the Cross. Therefore, serving Him is no longer a heavy burden but a joyful and an exciting adventure. In a personal relationship with the Lord, the yoke of service becomes easy and the burden of responsibility is light, for He carries the full weight of it upon His shoulders. Like a young child, the believers are fully dependent on Him who provides for their every need. Therefore, they are carefree with no anxieties about life.

In the natural, parents are to be like shepherds to their children. They carry the weight and responsibility of caring for their children's well being. Gradually, they learn from their parents how to take on responsibilities for themselves and others. Moreover, a stable Christian family learns how to work and play together in peace and harmony under the guidance of the Holy Spirit. Time is reserved for a long, restful vacation in a quiet natural setting of parks, beaches, and mountains. During their vacation, the family creates joyful memories of being together. Moreover, wise parents create opportunities to instruct children in their spiritual, intellectual, emotional, and social growth. Sadly, too often many parents find little or no time with their children who feel abandoned and neglected. Work comes first in their busy schedules.

In America, no one is able to endure the constant stress and pressures of a workaholic society. Labor without frequent times for recreation can break down one's physical, emotional, and spiritual well being. Furthermore, sleep deprivation causes dementia, premature aging, and disease. Driven by an overbearing desire to succeed in a high technological society, many Americans have become more and more stressed and isolated, lacking meaningful relationships with God and one another. Physical and spiritual rest is even more elusive for those who insist on getting a head. What comfort can be found in attaining goals such as fame or fortune? Sadly, the most miserable people on earth seem to be the "rich and famous." In contrast, those who find rest on the Sabbath are blessed and fortunate, for godliness with contentment is great gain! Therefore, the Lord of the Sabbath set aside a day of rest for the benefit of humanity

A Closer View of Humanity in Paradise Genesis Two

> This is the history of the heavens and the earth when they were created in the day that the Lord God made the earth and the heavens before any plant of the field was in earth and before any herb of the field had grown. For the Lord hadnot caused it to rain on the earth, and there was no man to till the ground. But a mist went up from the earth and watered the whole face of the ground.
>
> Genesis 2:4, 5.

Elleh toldot (Strong's # 8435 *Toldot* - Hebrew noun meaning: generations = account of man and his descendents) introduces a new narrative in the history of humanity for it denotes "generations", "this is the account of" "this is the family of"[30] In the second chapter of Genesis, the main focus of the creation history shifts from the physical realm to the creation of humanity. [31] In Genesis 1:28, 29, God commanded Adam and Eve to extend His rule over the earth:

> Be fruitful and increase in number; fill the earth and subdue it. Rule over the fish of the sea And the birds of the air and over every living creature that moves on the ground. I give you Every seed-bearing plant on the face of the whole earth and every tree

---

[30] Raymond B. Dillard and Tremper Longman III, *An Introduction to the Old Testament.* (Grand Rapids, Michigan: Zondervan, 1994), 48.

[31] Hugh Ross, *The Genesis Question: Scientific Advances and the Accuracy of Genesis.* (Colorado Springs, Colorado: Navpress Publishing Group, 1998), 69, 70.

Kathleen Martinez

that has fruit with seed in it. They will be yours for food.

At the time of their creation, Elohim gave the male and the female His divine mandate to care for all living creatures swarming in the sea, flying high above the sky, and teeming on the entire face of the earth. Moreover, God provided every seed- bearing plant and fruit trees for food. Green plants are basis of the food chain for mankind and animals. In the Garden of Eden, lush vegetation was irrigated by a mist or streams. (Strong's # 108 *Ed* is the Hebrew noun for streams). Furthermore, the clouds as water vapor were created in the sky on the second day, bringing forth abundant showers of rain (Genesis 1:6, 7; Job 36: 27, 28). Evidence of ancient rain falling on the earth has been observed by geologists. (Strong's #4305 *matar* is the Hebrew noun for rain or any form of precipitation). Splash patterns of raindrops on sedimentary deposits reveal that rain had been falling for millions of years before humanity appeared on earth. [32]

---

[32] Ibid., 72, 73.

Creation of Man from the Dust of the Ground

"And the Lord God formed man of the dust of the ground and breathed into his nostrils the breath of life and man became a living being."   Genesis 2:7

Like a potter who forms a vessel out of clay, the Lord God fashioned Adam from the dust of the ground. (Isaiah 29:16; Jeremiah 18:4) (*Yatsar Strong's # 3335* a Hebrew verb to form and fashion). (*'aphar* Strong's 6083 a Hebrew noun denoting the dry earth,dust, ashes). (*Adamah Strong's* #127 a Hebrew noun for earth, ground, land). Through an act of love, the Lord designed and fashioned the body of Adam as a unique reflection of Himself in the physical realm. Why? Through the creation of his human anatomy from the dust of the ground, the Lord created a portrait of Himself so that Adam would know Him in an intimate relationship.[33] Adam was created with a heart to love God, a willing mind to serve Him, and uplifted hands that offered Him praise, glory, and honor. Daily, Adam grew in knowledge and wisdom, learning more about His creation, and all living creatures. Through the natural realm of his Creation, the Lord God divulged the spiritual truths about the noble character and purpose of his Kingdom. As Adam learned to obey His Voice, and grow in the knowledge of His ways, the Father bestowed upon him divine authority to rule and reign as His representative on earth. God extend His Hands to provide, protect, and maintain the biosphere as a pure and stable environment for the health and well being of all living things. Everything that He had created was under the stewardship of humanity, who reflected His goodness, grace,

---

[33] Kenneth Ulmar, *In His Image: An Intimate Reflection of God.* (New Kensington, PA.: Whitaker House, 2005)., 14,18.

power, wisdom, knowledge, and understanding of His Kingdom of truth and righteousness.

Moreover, the Spirit of God breathed the breath of life into the nostrils of Adam and he became a living soul. (Genesis 2:7) [34] *(Nephesh* Strong's # 5315, a Hebrew feminine noun: soul, life, person, self, living being, desire, appetite, emotion, and passion). When God breathed His breath in man, He imparted the gift of His eternal life. Moreover, Adam became a living soul as a unique person and a self receiving divine wisdom of mind and an understanding heart. "But there is a spirit in man. And the breath of the Almighty gives him understanding" (Job 32:8). "Who has put wisdom in the mind? Or who has given understanding to the heart?" (Job 38:36). Thus, as an amazing creation, Adam possessed the capacity to commune with the Spirit of God, and comprehend His thoughts and His ways. Moreover, Elohim continues to create all human beings with special gifts and talents. All children are born with an amazing potential to impact the lives of people in their environment for the Kingdom of God. Moreover, in the sight of Father God, His sons and daughters have immeasurable value and dignity, for He made them in His own image and likeness. Their worth is far greater than silver or gold. Therefore, Christ gave His life through the shedding of His own Blood to bring redemption to all who believe in Him as Lord and Savior. "And this is the testimony: that God has given us eternal life and this life is in His Son. He who has the Son has life" (I John 5:11,12). "These things I have written to you who believe in the Name of the Son of God that you may know that you have eternal life."

---

[34] Ibid., 92,93.

The Garden of Eden

> The Lord God planted a garden, eastward in Eden,
> and there He put the man whom He had formed.
> And out of the ground the Lord God made every
> tree grow that is pleasant to the sight and good for
> food. The Tree of Life was also in the midst of the
> garden, and the tree of the knowledge of good and
> evil. Now a river went out of Eden to water the
> garden, and from there it parted and became four
> riverheads.   Genesis 2: 8-10

The Garden of Eden is a territory, located east of Israel in
Mesopotamia or Arabia [35] (*gan be-eden* Strong's #5731proper noun,
derived from *eden* Strong's#5730, a Hebrew noun denoting luxury,
dainty, delight). The biblical text states that a river that watered the
garden flowed from Eden and divided into four headstreams that
are identified as the Pishon, the Gihon, the Tigris and the Euphrates
rivers. However, the Pishon and Gihon rivers, having altered their
course over time, can only be observed from space. Photographs
taken by satellites reveal that the dry riverbeds could have been the
rivers described in Genesis, running throughout the south-central
Mesopotamian plain.[36]. Moreover, the Garden of Eden is a "delight"
that God Himself planted as an ornate paradise. (*pardes* Strong's #
6508 denotes preserve, park ; a loan word barrowed from Persian,
denoting a garden with fruit trees and costly plants). A wealthy
King of Jerusalem seeking pleasure in his life stated, "I made for

---

[35] Jack W. Hayford, executive editor, *New Spirit-Filled Life Bible: Kingdom
Equipping Through the Power of the Word (NKJV)*. (Nashville, TN : Thomas
Nelson, Inc., 2002)., 7.

[36] Hugh Ross, *The Genesis Question: Scientific Advances and the Accuracy of
Genesis.* (Colorado Springs, Colorado: NavPress Publishing Group).77, 78.

myself orchards and gardens, (*pardesim*), and I planted all kinds of fruit trees in them" (Ecclesiastes 2:5). Lord God planted a luxurious garden in Eden with an abundance of fruit trees to gratify the eyes of humanity. In the midst of the garden was the Tree of Life, producing food for the health and nourishment for all living beings. Moreover, this affluent land was enriched with valuable gold, bdellium, and onyx stones (Genesis 2:12).

> Then the Lord God took the man and put him in the Garden of Eden to tend and keep it. And the Lord God commanded the man, saying, "Of every tree of the garden, you may freely eat; but of the tree of the knowledge of good and evil, you shall not eat, for in the for in the day that you eat of it, you shall surely die.   Genesis 2:15-17. (NKJV)

The Lord God placed Adam in the Garden of Eden to work and till the ground (*abad* # Strong's 5647 a Hebrew verb denoting work, serve). Furthermore, he preserved and cared for His garden. (*shamar* # Strong's 8104 a Hebrew verb denoting keep, watch,preserve). Thus, Adam was given charge over the garden as a steward entrusted with His property. "The earth is the Lord's and all its fullness, the world and those who dwell therein" Psalm 24:1. Today, the work of cultivation and the care of the earth is still a divine mandate for all of Humanity to observe. The Lord God holds all men responsible for their failure to properly farm and preserve the land. Now, physical and spiritual pollution is the major cause of death and destruction of all living beings. The destruction of the environment often brings dire and severe consequences of forest fires, droughts, floods, and hurricanes.

Furthermore, as a sign of His Sovereignty and Lordship over all the earth and its inhabitants, the Lord God issued a command forbidding Adam to eat from the Tree of the Knowledge of Good and Evil. Although Adam was free to eat from all the other trees of the garden, Lord God warned him that the consequences of partaking of the forbidden fruit of the Tree of Knowledge would be physical and spiritual death. Disobedience of God's prohibition would cost Adam eternal life. "The wages of sin is death" (Romans 6:23). The punishment of eating the forbidden fruit would be eternal separation from God, and the forfeiture of his dominion over all living things: the plants and the animals on the land, the sea, and in the sky.(Genesis 1:26 As their earthly caretaker, Adam was given the responsibility of naming all of the animals. They were his companions, requiring his love, time, and attention.

> And the Lord God said, "It is not good that man should be alone: I will make a helper comparable to him. Out of the ground the Lord God formed every beast of the field and every bird of the air, and brought them to Adam to see what he would call them. And whatever Adam called each living creature, that was its name. So Adam gave names to all the cattle, to the birds of the air, and to every beast of the field. Genesis 2:18-20.

Through diligent study and close observation of every creature dwelling on the land, soaring in the air and swimming in the sea, Adam was exercising his stewardship over them, classifying all living things according to their physical characteristics and behavior. As Adam gained valuable knowledge through his observation and care for the animals and their environment, the Lord God was watching over him to bless and prosper him. In the process of observation, Adam grew daily in his knowledge of the greatness and the goodness of his heavenly Father. However, Adam felt alone and needed a helper comparable to him.

Kathleen Martinez

The Creation of Eve as Helper and Companion

And the Lord God caused a deep sleep to fall on Adam, and He slept; and He took one of his ribs, and closed up the flesh in its place. Then the rib which the Lord God had taken from man, He made into a woman and He brought her to the man.

Genesis 2:21, 22.

The Lord God, the Master builder, fashioned a woman from the side of Adam (*banah* Strong's # 1129 a Hebrew verb denoting build or fashion) (*tselah* Strong's # 6763 A Hebrew noun denoting side, rib). He caused him to fall into a deep sleep. And from his side, the Lord God removed some tissue from which He fashioned a woman. The biopsy provided a blueprint from the cells of Adam to construct a complete new individual as his equal, for she came from his side. When the Lord God brought her to him, Adam recognized that she was his partner who was a comparable extension of himself. Therefore, he exclaimed with great delight, "This is now bone of my bones and flesh of my flesh and she shall be called woman for she was taken out of man" (Genesis 2:23, 24). Unlike the animals who were soul creatures, the woman was a spiritual being, made in the image and likeness of God. She possessed a capacity to have an intimate, harmonious relationship with God and her husband. As a couple, they had greater power for the woman was designed to be his helper and military ally[37] (*Ezer* Strong's # 5828 a Hebrew noun for helper). Together, man and woman would have an equal share of the responsibility of ruling over creation as representatives of

---

[37] Hugh Ross, *The Genesis Question Scientific Advances and the Accuracy of Genesis*. (Colorado Springs, Colorado: NavPress Publishing Group).76

God's Kingdom on earth. Looking to God as their help, they would conquer, and maintain their dominion over all spiritual and natural forces. Finally, God the Father established the sacred institution of brought them together to be united in marriage.

> Therefore, a man shall leave his father and mother
> and be joined to his wife and they shall be one flesh.
>
> Genesis 2:24

In the Garden of Eden, God established the institution of marriage between a man and a woman to fulfill His desire to create for Himself a family on earth as reflection of the love and unity between the Father, the Son, and the Holy Spirit. Created in the image and likeness of God, a man and his wife are triune beings with a body, soul, and spirit. They become one flesh just as God is one. What is the meaning of being one? In Deuteronomy 6: 4, Moses speaking to Israel declared, "The Lord our God, the Lord is One" ('*echad* Strong's # 259 Hebrew word, an adjective, number one). Just as three Persons of the Godhead are united together as One, Christian couples are joined together in holy matrimony cleaving to one another (*debaq* Strong's # 1692 a Hebrew verb that denotes to cling, cleave, keep close). Through making a lifelong commitment to one another before God, they declare their vows to be faithful to one another. Therefore, Christian marriage is a sacred covenantal bond, an intimate relationship designed to reflect the love and unity between Christ and the Church. (Ephesians 5: 22-33) The overall purpose of His plan of redemption is to restore the original harmony and unity between Himself as Creator Elohim and humanity. The prayer of Jesus Christ is that His disciples "may all be one as You the Father are in Me and I, in You that they also maybe *one* in Us that the world may believe that You sent Me" (John 17:21).

In the sacred bond of a marriage covenant, a man and his wife reflect the love and unity of the Godhead, for they remain faithful and true to one another as lifelong partners, warmed by deep friendship, tender affection, and close physical proximity. Love and unity is the cry of God.

> Two are better than one because they have a good reward for their labor. For if they Fall, one will lift up his companion. But woe to him who is alone when he falls, for he has no one to help him up. Again, if two lie down, they will be kept warm; but how can one be warm alone? Though one may be overpowered by another, two can withstand him. And a threefold cord is not quickly broken.
> Ecclesiastes 4: 9-12.

Unfortunately, the threefold cord of unity between man, woman, and God would be broken. Through embracing the lies of the deceptive spirit of Satan, they doubted and questioned the goodness and fidelity of God. Questioning His integrity would lead to temptation and disobedience of His Word. Consequently, their relationship with their heavenly Father and one another would be shattered. Moreover, the sin and rebellion of Adam against the Truth of God's Word brought darkness, sin, and death into the world. However, Elohim had already established before the foundation of the world, His plan of redemption that would restore the perfect harmonious relationship of love and unity between humanity and their Creator.

Partaking of the Forbiden Fruit Leading Down the Path of Destruction - Genesis Three

To the young and naïve, Wisdom of God speaks a word of warning in Proverbs:

Do not enter the path of the wicked and do not walk in the way of evil.
Avoid it, do not travel on it; Turn away from it and pass on.   Proverb 4:14

Now therefore, listen to me, my children
Pay attention to the words of my mouth
Do not let your heart turn aside to her ways
Do not stray into her paths;
For she has cast down many wounded
And all who were slain by her were strong men.
Her house is the way to hell, descending to the chambers of death.   Proverbs 7: 21

There is a way that seems right to a man,
But its end is the way of death.   Proverb 14:12

In the early 1960's and the 1970's, American youth rose up in rebellion, rejecting the materialism of their parents who were driven by their quest for wealth and success in their place of work. At this time, they bitterly opposed the industrial- military establishment that had led America into the Vietnam War. Therefore, being disenchanted by the values of their corrupt government, along with the injustice of racism, and inequalities between men and women, they left home seeking an alternative lifestyle of drugs and sexual relationships outside of marriage. Moreover, they questioned the validity and relevance of fundamental Judeo-Christian principles and values. Also, embracing the philosophy of relativism caused American society to reject the traditional Christian faith that acknowledges God as the Sovereign Lord of the universe. For more than half a century, an apostate culture has rebelled against God, turning away from His laws as universal standards of justice and righteousness. Ironically, Americans may admit that absolute laws of physics govern the universe. However, spiritual laws are considered outdated and irrelevant in contemporary society. Therefore, the pursuit of truth has become more and more subjective as the present generation raises the question: Why not determine one's own beliefs and philosophy of life? The lifestyle of the American elite is predominately self-centered often experimenting with drugs, exotic music, and sexual perversions. Since the mid 1960's, American society has steadily gone down the path of destruction and immorality.

Nevertheless, the Spirit of the Lord was pursuing and drawing many college-aged people into His Kingdom in another movement known as the "Jesus movement". This timely move of God was His divine response to the earnest intercession of many prayer-warriors standing in the gap for their lost children. Many parents fell on their knees in desperation, seeking the Lord for a new move of God that would bring their children deliverance and salvation.

Was the "Jesus Movement" just another fad? No, for young people discovered that Christ was the One who filled emptiness in their hearts. At the critical time in their life, college-aged students were actively pursuing their true identity and purpose in life. Longing for forgiveness, unconditional love, and acceptance, they received Jesus Christ as their Lord and Savior. As sons and daughters of their heavenly Father, they were no longer spiritual orphans controlled by the forces of darkness. Rejoicing in their new lifestyle in Christ, they began their new life walking in the Spirit of God and in the Light of His Word. The Word of God was the lamp that shed light guiding their steps onto the path of righteousness. Consequently, new believers gained total confidence that they stood before the throne of God in the righteousness of Christ. Moreover, as children of God, they received His promise of eternal life. "And this is the testimony: that God has given us eternal life, and this life is in His Son. He who has the Son has life; he who does not have the Son of God does not have life" (I John 5:11, 12). For the followers of Christ, the Christian walk was full of love, joy, and peace. They delighted in the law of the Lord. Meditating on it day and night, they became effective witnesses for Christ. Moreover, they were filled with the Holy Spirit who imparted spiritual gifts such as faith, miracles, healing and deliverance. The Sword of Truth was their offensive weapon for combating the tactics of Satan and tearing down the rulers of darkness. Since the Fall of Man in the Garden of Eden, the main target of Satan has been the young and naïve.

The Tragic Fall of Man

In the Garden of Eden, *Chava*, the young wife of Adam took daily pleasure exploring her habitat, the Garden of Eden, a paradise filled with a vast array of fruit trees. Furthermore, she was attracted to the beauty of Tree of the Knowledge of Good and Evil, for it is heavy laden with luxuriant foliage, bearing luscious fruit. Chava was particularly drawn to its fragrance. Suddenly, a serpent (*HaNahash*) who was more crafty and shrewd than all of the animals of the field appeared on the branch of a tree. (*Arum*, Strong's # 6195, a Hebrew adjective that denotes crafty, shrewd, and sensible). This beautiful creature struck up a serious debate in an alluring conversation with a question, "Has God indeed said, 'You shall not eat of every tree of the garden'?" (Genesis 3:1) In a reply, Chava answered the question stating, "We may eat the fruit of the trees of the garden; but of the fruit of the tree which is in the midst of the garden, God has said, 'You shall not eat it, nor touch it, lest you die.'" Her initial response came from the heart, for God had given her a conscience to discern right from wrong. However, she added an additional prohibition to His Word stating, "You shall not eat it nor shall you touch it lest you die." Moreover, Chava continued to converse with her enemy, exposing herself to his sinister spirit. She was unaware of his tactic convincing her to question the integrity and goodness of God, and to break His commandments. Moreover, his overall purpose was to sever her relationship with God her heavenly Father. Through his smooth speech and supreme craftiness, he was able to draw her into the snare of deception that would lead her down the path of death and destruction. The moment that she partook of the forbidden fruit, her eyes would be opened. She would become like God, knowing both good and evil. Moreover, he told another lie that the Lord God was withholding His amazing knowledge and wisdom. Why should she submit to God when she could have unlimited freedom and independence? Unfortunately, Chava failed to stand firmly upon the Word God and take seriously His warnings. Instead, she listened to the voice of the serpent who boldly contradicted God. "You will not surely die." (Genesis 3:4) The lie is the only resource that the evil one possesses in his assault against the Truth of God's Word. In John 8:44, Jesus called Satan a liar. He spoke to unbelieving Jews stating that their father is the devil and he, "does not stand in the truth, because there is no truth in him. When he speaks a lie, he speaks from his own resources, for he is a liar and the father of it." The liar convinced Chava that God was denying her right to govern herself, and to live her life as she pleased. Why not reject His instructions and restrictions? Self- reliance seemed to be the right path to follow. Through his distortion and perversion of the Truth, evil appeared to be good and harmless. "There is a way that seems right to a man, but its end is the way of death" (Proverb 14:12).

Her disobedience opened the door to sin and the punishment of eternal death. Chava became a victim who was easily persuaded by the power of temptation: the lust of the flesh (the tree was good for food), the lust of the eyes (pleasant to the eyes), and the pride of life (made one wise). "For all that is in the world— the lust of the flesh, the lust of the eyes, and the pride of life— is not of the Father but is of the world" (I John 2:16).

Does the tragic story of the Fall of Adam and Chava continue to unfold in the world today? Yes. Today, western nations have fallen into spiritual decline. Liberal judges, educators, the media, and the American elite have made it politically correct to remove God from all areas of public life and persecute true Christians who stand for the sanctity of life, and the traditional marriage between and man and a woman. Moreover, America is no longer a Christian nation for many Americans are ensnared by Satan: committing fornication, seeking unwarranted pleasure, and being under the influence of drugs and alcohol trying to escape reality of their spiritual poverty.

Unfortunately, friends and family often lead children into a life of addiction and crime. Their tragic example is a reenactment of the sin of Adam and Chava in the Garden of Eden. After Chava partook of the forbidden fruit, she offered it to her husband. Standing nearby, Adam did not attempt to avert her disobedience nor did he resist temptation. In the interest of pleasing his wife, he listened to her voice rather than the Voice of the Spirit. With his eyes wide open, Adam sinned. "Therefore just as through one man sin entered the world and death through sin and thus death spread to all men because all sinned" (Romans 5:12).

Suddenly, Adam and his wife experienced grave and tragic consequences of their sin. (Genesis 3:6; I John 2:16). Immediately, they faced the grim reality of spiritual death and their broken relationship with God and one another. Thus, as the separator, the liar succeeded in bringing about a sharp division between heaven and earth and a spirit of hostility in humanity toward God. "Sin acts as a separator". [38] Today, humanity partakes of the poisonous fruit of the tree of the knowledge of good and evil causing hate and violence to penetrate and destroy the unity of America at an alarming pace, separating men, women, and children from God, their only Source of eternal life, love, and unity.

> "Blessed is the man who listens to me, watching daily at my gates, waiting at the posts of my doors. For whoever finds Me finds life, and obtains favor from the Lord. But he who sins against Me wrongs his own soul; All those who hate Me love death"
> Proverbs 8:34-36.

Furthermore, when the eyes of Adam and Chava were opened, they saw that they were naked, for they were no longer clothed with the glory and presence of God. In vain, they attempted to cover up

---

[38] Perry Stone, *How a Mountain of Fire and a Rebellious Cherub Altered History in Heaven and on Earth Chronicles of the Sacred Mountain: Revealing The Mysteries of Heaven's Past, Present and Future.* (Cleveland, TN: Voice of Evangelism Outreach Ministries, 2015). 66

their nakedness, sewing fig leaves for a covering. Unfortunately, their garments were insufficient to hide their guilt and shame in the sight of the Lord God. Upon hearing "the sound of His footsteps walking in the garden in the cool of the day", they hid themselves from His presence among the trees of the garden" (Genesis 3:8). As their loving Father, the Lord drew near to be present with His children at the very moment that they fell into sin and darkness. He would not abandon His children in their darkest hour of need.

> Am I a God near at hand, says the Lord, And not a God afar off? Can anyone hide himself in secret places so I shall not see him? Says the Lord; Do I not fill heaven and earth says the Lord.   Jeremiah 23:23, 24

In His great love and compassion for them, the Lord God immediately came down to pursue them in the cool of the day calling out, "Where are you?" Fearful of hearing His Voice and standing naked in His Presence, Adam attempted to hide from the Lord. Now, he was overwhelmed with painful emotions of guilt and shame. Shaken with fear, Adam responded to His heavenly Father, "I heard Your Voice in the garden, and I was afraid because I was naked and I hid myself" (Verse 10). Urging Adam to confess his disobedience to his command, Father God interrogated him, "Who told you that you were naked? Have you eaten from the tree of which I commanded you that you should not eat?" (Verse 11) Not willing to take responsibility for his own actions, Adam blamed Chava for his disobedience saying, "The woman whom you gave to be with me, she gave me of the tree and I ate" (Verse 12). Turning to Chava, God confronted her, "What is this you have done?" Her response was to pass the blame for her disobedience unto the serpent, "The serpent deceived me and I ate" (Verse 13). Lord God directed His attention on the serpent and passed His sentence of judgment on the "serpent of old, called the Devil (Satan) who deceives the whole world" (Revelation 12:9).

Because you have done this, you are cursed more than all cattle, And more than every beast of the field; On your belly you shall go, And you shall eat dust all the days of your life. And I will put enmity between you and the woman and between your seed and her Seed; 'He shall bruise your head and you shall bruise His heel

Genesis 3: 14, 15.

For deceiving Chava, causing her to eat the forbidden fruit in violation of His command, the Lord God delivered His sentence of judgment upon the serpent. What was the judgment of God upon the deceiver? The Lord God declared that he would crawl on his belly in the lowest degree of abasement and humiliation, eating the dust of the ground for all his days on earth. Although the true identity of the serpent was not revealed in the Garden of Eden, he would be unmasked later. According to Revelation 12:9, the serpent in the Garden of Eden was the devil (Satan). What was his agenda on earth? What was his true identity and ministry in the past when God created His universe?

According to the prophet Isaiah, before the creation of Adam and Chava, God had created His angelic hosts. Chief among the angels was Lucifer (the Hebrew word for *heylel* translated as "son of the morning" (Isaiah 14:12).[39] He was an anointed cherub, who held the highest position as the guardian in the presence of God. Along with the heavenly host of angels who observed Elohim lay the foundation of the earth with shouts of joy was Lucifer.

Where were you when I laid the foundations of the earth? ...Or who laid its cornerstone when the

---

[39] Perry Stone, *How a Mountain of Fire and a Rebellious Cherub Altered History in Heaven and on Earth Chronicles of the Sacred Mountain: Revealing The Mysteries of Heaven's Past, Present and Future.* (Cleveland, TN: Voice of Evangelism Outreach Ministries, 2015). 71

morning stars sang together and all the sons of God
shouted for joy.   Job 38:4-7

Now there was a day when the sons of God came
to present themselves before the Lord and Satan
was also among them. And the Lord said to Satan,
"From where do you come?" So Satan answered the
Lord and said," From going to and fro on the earth
and from walking back and forth on it" Job 1:6, 7.

Satan was among the angelic beings that came to present
themselves before the Lord. Although he was a fallen angel, Satan
was free to go wherever he pleased, roaming to and fro on the earth.
Moreover, during the days of Job, he is portrayed as the accuser of
men. As the watcher of men, he sought to uncover their faults and
weakness to bring them down to destruction for God had cast him
down from his high position as the guardian in His glorious presence?
Why? According to the prophet Ezekiel, as Lucifer, he was "perfect in
all his ways until "iniquity" was found in him (Ezekiel 28:15).

You were the anointed cherub who covers; I
established you. You were on the Holy Mountain
of God; You walked back and forth in the midst of
fiery stones. You were perfect in all your ways from
the day you were created, till iniquity was found in
you…Therefore I cast you as a profane thing out
of the mountain of God. And I destroyed you, O
covering cherub, from the midst of the fiery stones.
Your heart was lifted up because of your beauty. You
corrupted your wisdom for the sake of your splendor
I cast you to the ground.   Ezekiel 28: 14-17

How did sin enter into God's universe? Sin first entered into the
universe as pride rose up in the heart of Lucifer. The spirit of vanity

took hold of him when he began to worship himself, focusing on his beauty and splendor. His pride and arrogance caused him to rebel against the Lord God, the King of Heaven and earth. Moreover, he desired to rule over God's universe by casting Him down from His throne. As Lucifer became focused upon himself, he coveted the power, the glory, and the splendor of God. Therefore, God brought judgment against him and cast him out of the Mountain of His Kingdom. In retaliation, Satan began to plot his revenge against God. In five bold declarations, he revealed his desire to be like the Most High:

> I will ascend into heaven, I will exalt my throne above the stars of God, I will also sit on the mount of the congregation on the farthest sides of the north; I will ascend above the heights of the clouds, I will be like the Most High   Isaiah 14:13-14.

In the Garden of Eden, Satan formulated a plan to usurp power and authority that God had bestowed upon His sons whom God had created in His exact image and likeness. They were appointed to be representatives of His Kingdom. On the day of their creation, Elohim blessed them, issuing His mandate to be fruitful, multiply, fill the earth, and subdue it (Genesis 1:28). With deep animosity, Satan loathed these earthly creatures for they reflected the glory of God. Now, Satan refused to be subdued by men. Through deception, the enemy would cause them to fall away from God in order to seize their dominion on earth.

What would be his strategy to regain his power on earth? Satan would attack the character of God, accusing Him of being a liar, who was not worthy of their love, trust, and obedience. Adam and Chava would fall for his deception, rebel against God, and thus surrender their divine right to reign on earth. Thus, Satan would establish his rule over them as the "god of this world". Through the original sin of Adam, the spirits of Death and Hell (mentioned as the fourth seal in Revelation 6:8) were released with their demonic power to kill and destroy all men. Now, the dark shadow of evil dominated the whole earth throughout human history.

However, in the eyes of Elohim, the loss of paradise would not be forever. Before the Fall, the Lord God had created His own plan to deliver humanity from sin and death and create a new paradise. For the vision of God was to dwell with men in a New Heaven and a New Earth for all eternity.

> Behold the tabernacle of God is with men and He
> will dwell with them, and they shall be His people.
> God himself will be with them and be their God.
> Revelation 21:3.

Kathleen Martinez

God's Plan of Redemption

> And I will put enmity (*,eybah* Strong's # 342 a Hebrew noun denoting hatred and personal hostility ; from,*ayab* Strong's # 340 A Hebrew verb to be an enemy) between you and the woman and between your seed and her Seed; 'He shall bruise your head and you shall bruise His heel.'   Genesis 3:15.

The Fall of Adam and Chava created in all men a spirit of lawlessness separating them from the Source of Life. Furthermore, humanity was divided by hatred and violence because of pride and selfish ambition. Throughout the entire span of human history, men lived in a cosmic war zone in which a raging battle would ensue between the forces of Good (God's Kingdom) and Evil (Satan's pseudo kingdom). Chaos, oppression, and spiritual darkness would dominate earth for thousands of years. "Therefore, just as through one man sin entered the world and death through sin and thus death spread to all men, because of sin" (Romans 5:12). As the consequence of the sin of Adam, all of creation was under the sentence death. Moreover, Satan subjected all flesh under his power of death.

Nevertheless, there was good news for all men who would put their trust in the Lord Jesus Christ. Through the Messiah, Father God promised to save them from sin and death, and offer them His gift of eternal life. "For the wages of sin is death, but the gift of God is eternal life in Christ Jesus" (Romans 6:23). In anticipation of the Fall of Adam, God had appointed the Lamb of God to be slain before the foundation of the earth (Revelation 13:8). Before the creation of the world, the Son of God was willing to submit Himself to His Father's plan of redemption. Out of love for His Father and humanity, He was willing to lay down His life to save sinners. Jesus declared that He is "the Good Shepherd gives His life for the sheep" (John 10:11). Through His death on the cross on which his heel would be bruised, Christ, the Seed of the woman, would defeat and destroy the kingdom of Satan, crushing his head. Through His death on the cross and His resurrection, Jesus would destroy death, the last enemy of men. "Death is swallowed up in victory" (I Corinthians 15:54).

Refusing to abandon His creation to His adversary Satan, Father God would send His only Son into the world to seek and save the lost. How would He enter into this world? He would be incarnated as a perfect human being conceived by a virgin. "Therefore the Lord Himself will give you a sign: Behold the virgin shall conceive and bear a Son and shall call His Name Immanuel" (Isaiah 7:14). His Name would be called Immanuel, (God with us). For thousands of years, the world would wait in great expectation for the fulfillment of God's promise to send the Messiah, the Seed of the woman. "Now to Abraham and his Seed were the promises made. He does not say "And to seeds" as of many, but as one, And to your Seed" who is Christ" (Galatians3:16). In his letter to the Galatians, Paul alluded to the first promise that the Lord God gave in the Garden of Eden to Adam and Chava and their offspring. Genesis 3:15 is the *Protoevangelium*, the first messianic prophecy in the Old Testament [40] Faithful to His promise of deliverance, the purpose of the Son of God would surely be accomplished. Through His death, burial, and resurrection, He would destroy the works of the devil. "He who sins is of the devil, for the devil has sinned from the beginning. For this purpose the Son of God was manifested, that He might destroy the works of the devil" (I John 3:8). As their Messiah, Jesus Christ would set men free from the power of Satan who inflicted them with pain, sickness, and death.

---

[40] Jack Hayford, Executive Editor, *New Spirit-Filled Bible: Kingdom Equipping Through the Power of the Word*
(Nashville, TN: Thomas Nelson Publishers, 2002). 9

Kathleen Martinez

The Conseqences of Sin

God sets the solitary in families. He brings out those who are bound into prosperity;

But the rebellious dwell in a dry land. Psalm 68:6

Good understanding gains favor, but the way of the transgressors is hard.   Proverbs 13:15

An evil man seeks only rebellion;
Therefore a cruel messenger will be sent against him
                                                    Proverb 17:11

To the woman He said, "I will greatly multiply your sorrow and your conception;
In pain you shall bring forth children. Your desire shall be for your husband, and He shall rule over you."   Genesis 3:16

The consequence of Chava partaking of the forbidden fruit would propagate pain in conception and child birth. ('*itstsabown* Strong's # 6093 a Hebrew noun denoting pain and toil both in agriculture and travail). Ironically, the blessing of conceiving and bearing children would be associated with the curse of pain in labor. Furthermore, the desire of Chava would be for her husband. (*tashuwqah* Strong's #8669 a longing of a woman for a man). Looking to her husband to satisfy her needs would cause conflict and strife in their marital relationship. In contrast, the wise woman would seek the Lord as her Creator- Husband. She has confidence that He provides for all her needs, and her spirit of rest brings peace and harmony in her home. "The Lord is my Shepherd, I shall not be in want" (Psalm 23:1) She lacks no good thing. Moreover, trusting in the Word of the Lord, she is able to resist the temptation of fear and rejection. For she knows that fear and torment come from Satan. The love of God casts out all fear. "For God has not given us a spirit of fear, but of power, and of love and of a sound mind (II Timothy 1:7). Facing the challenge of child birth, a mother can rely on the promise of God. "Nevertheless, she will be saved in child bearing if they continue in faith, love, and holiness, with self control" (I Timothy 2:15). No longer does she strive in her relationships to control others for her own advantage nor for the purpose of gaining recognition for good works. Instead, both she and her husband give freely of themselves to care for the needs of others, using their spiritual gifts to advance the Kingdom of God. Surely, the Lord God will honor and reward them for their faithfulness in the home, the church, and the community! Moreover, all Christians have through the Spirit of God power and authority to stand firmly against the onslaught of Satan's works.

As the husband of Chava, Adam failed to protect her from deception. Moreover, his sin and disobedience opened the door to a life of sweat and toil.

> To Adam He said, "Because you have heeded the voice of your wife, and have eaten from the Tree of which I commanded you, saying 'You shall not eat of it':
>
> "Cursed is the ground for your sake; In toil you shall eat of it all the days of your life. Both thorns and thistles shall it shall bring forth for you. And you shall eat the herb of of the field. In the sweat of your face, you shall eat bread till you return to the ground. For out of it you were taken. For dust you are and to dust you shall return   Genesis 3:17-19

Kathleen Martinez

Due to the sin of Adam, all humanity would experience oppressive pain and suffering. The Word of the Lord had been a warning of the consequences of sin. The life of the transgressor would be hard, and that the rebellious would dwell in a dry land. Because Adam listened to the voice of his wife Chava, the Lord cursed the ground. Cultivating the earth would no longer be an easy and rewarding occupation. By the sweat of his brow, he would raise crops to provide bread for himself and family until the day of his death. His body would ultimately perish and return to the dust of the ground from which the Lord God had formed him. Moreover, an abundance of thorns and thistles would spring up overtaking the productivity of the land. Moreover, thorns and thistles would be symbolic of the heavy burden of daily life on earth. Tribulation would exist because lawless men live in a constant state of rebellion against the Lord God. "The heart of men is deceitful above all things and desperately wicked. Who can know it? I the Lord, search the heart, I test the mind, even to give every man according to his ways, according to the fruit of his doings" (Jeremiah 17:9, 10). The Lord God searches the hearts of men and tests their minds to reveal hidden their motives and desires. He is acquainted with all their wicked ways and will surely judge them according to their works on the Day of Judgment. How shall a man escape judgment who points the finger at others while he stands guilty before God the Righteous Judge?

> Do you think this, O man, you who judge those who practice such things and doing the same, that you will escape the judgment of God? Or do you despise the riches of His goodness, forbearance, and longsuffering, not knowing that the goodness of God leads you to repentance? But in accordance with your hardness and impenitent heart, you are treasuring up for yourself wrath in the day of wrath and revelation of the righteous judgment of God

who will render to each one according to his deeds.

Romans 2:3-6

Before issuing His judgment, God patiently pours out His goodness, hoping for the repentance of sinners. True to His divine nature, He displays His amazing forbearance, endurance, and longsuffering spirit toward the souls of men. Although the righteousness of God demands judgment of those who have transgressed His covenant, He continues to extend His mercy toward His people. "For I desire mercy and not sacrifice and the knowledge of God more than burnt offerings?" (Hosea 6:6) Furthermore, He provides garments of salvation to array His saints in His glory and righteousness.

Kathleen Martinez

His Institution of the Blood Sacrifice as Covering for Sin [41]

> "And Adam called his wife Chava because she was the mother of all living. Also for Adam and his wife, the Lord God made tunics of skin and clothed them"
> Genesis 3:20, 21.

In the Garden of Eden, God instituted the blood sacrifice in order to cover the nakedness of Adam and Chava. Providing them with garments of skin would require the sacrifice of an innocent animal. Moreover, the essential element of His redemptive covenants was the blood sacrifice. Throughout the Old Testament, the sacrifice of animals without blemish was the prototype of the blood sacrifice of the sinless Lamb of God. "For the life of the flesh is in the blood and I have given it to you upon the altar to make atonement for your souls, for it is the blood that makes atonement for the soul" (Leviticus 17:11) (*kaphar*, Strong's # 3722 Hebrew word that denotes to make atonement, cleanse, disannul, forgive, be merciful, pacify, pardon, pitch, purge away, put off, make reconciliation) "Without the shedding of Blood, there is no remission of sin" (Hebrews 9:22). (*Aphesis*, Strong's #859 Greek noun denoting: pardon, deliverance, forgiveness, liberty, remission.) What a dramatic demonstration of the love of the Father who offered up His only Son as the blood sacrifice for humanity. His substitutionary death paid in full the wages of sin. But until the remission of their sin, Adam and Chava would have to be barred from the Tree of Life.

---

[41] Jack Hayford Executive Ed, *New Spirit-Filled Life Bible*. (Nashville, TN: Thomas Nelson Publishers, 2002), 10.

Then the Lord God said, "Behold, the man has become like one of Us to know good and evil. And now, lest he put out his hand and take also of of the Tree of Life and eat and live forever"— Therefore the Lord God sent him out of the garden of Eden to till the ground from which he was taken. So He drove out the man and He placed cherubim at the east of the garden of Eden, and a flaming sword which turned every way to guard the way to the Tree of Life.   Genesis 3:22-24

After partaking of the Tree of Knowledge, the man became like Elohim knowing good and evil. Now Adam must not eat the fruit of the Tree of Life that was standing in the midst of the Garden of Eden. If he were to partake of it, Adam would live for all eternity in the state of sin, separated from God forever. To prevent this tragedy with no hope of redemption and reconciliation, the Lord God quickly cast him out of paradise to till the ground from which he was taken. In order to defend the way to the Tree of Life, He placed cherubim to stand guard wielding flaming swords that turn in all directions. While living outside of paradise, man clung onto the hope of redemption. Now the creation longs to be "delivered from the bondage of corruption into the glorious liberty of the children of God… the whole creation groans and labors with birth pangs until now" (Romans 8:21, 22). Suffering under the burden of sin, the physical universe cries out for deliverance. What will happen to the original creation of heaven and earth? The Lord God will not coexist with the old creation tainted by sin and rebellion. Therefore, He will destroy it and then create a new heaven and a new earth. "Now I saw a new heaven and a new earth for the first heaven and the first earth had passed away" (Revelation 21:1). As the redeemed of the Lord, a new humanity will live forever in paradise, having free access to the Tree of Life. "And he showed me a pure river of water of life clear as crystal, proceeding from the throne of God and of the

Lamb. In the middle of the street on either side of the river, was the Tree of Life" (Revelation 22:1, 2).

Sadly throughout history, humanity continued to fall deeper and deeper into spiritual darkness. For the original sin of Adam increased at an alarming rate and continued to cast its ominous shadow over the entire earth. When the relationship between God and humanity was severed by sin, man became a murderer.[42] When He formed him from the ground, God called the first man by the Hebrew name *Adam* that begins with the letter "*aleph.*" As the first letter of the Hebrew alphabet, *Aleph* represents God's eternal presence As the Head, Originator, Designer, and Creator of the Hebrew language and the universe, the Father would always be actively involved with humanity. Furthermore, *Aleph* symbolizes His intention to dwell with humanity in perfect harmony. Upon the fall of Adam, sin caused the *Aleph* to depart from humanity. If the first letter "A" is removed from the name Adam, the remaining letters spell "dam." The Hebrew word *dam* denotes blood" revealing the bloody nature of fallen humanity. Without *Aleph,* the peace of God ruling in his evil heart, man has become a belligerent animal that lives in a constant state of war. In the fourth chapter of Genesis, envy and uncontrolled anger drives Cain to commit the first murder.

---

[42] L. Grant Luton, *In His Own Words: Messianic Insights into the Hebrew Alphabet* (Uniontown, Ohio: Beth Tikkun Publishing,1999), 19.

Divergence in the First Family- Two Seeds –Godly (Seth) and Ungodly (Cain)

> Now Adam Knew Eve his wife and she conceived and bore Cain and said, "I have acquired a man from the Lord." Then she bore again, this time his name was Abel. Now Abel was a keeper of sheep, but Cain was a tiller of the ground. Genesis 4:1, 2.

In the early twentieth century, Marjorie Brown conceived and bore two sons, Hugh Henry Brown in 1906 and Marshall Roberts Brown in 1908. According to the highest standards of conduct of upper class society, Mrs. Brown was determined to raise her children to be well mannered gentlemen. At all times, they were to be on their best behavior, reflecting the morals and values of their parents. However, they did not always measure up to her high expectations. Therefore, on more than one occasion, she did not hesitate to employ unusual methods of discipline. While playing outside in plain sight of the neighbors, Hugh and Marshall engaged in a heated argument. In an uncontrolled fit of anger, the elder son began to throw rocks at his younger brother. Upon observing such outlandish behavior, their mother quickly ran outside, filled her apron with rocks, and began to cast them at her eldest son. Viewing this incident, the neighbors were in a state of shock. What possessed Mrs. Brown to act in such an undignified manner? Both her children were also taken back by the actions of their mother and pleaded with her to stop. Without pausing to consider her actions, a strong spirit of indignation took hold of her.

Approximately fifty years later, Mr. Marshall Brown relayed this story to his children to teach them about proper behavior in the home. As their father, he would not permit any form of verbal or physical violence. Peace and quietness in the home would be strictly observed. Unfortunately, his youngest daughter often rebelled and disrupted the household, losing her temper causing him shame and embarrassment. How would he deal with her without losing control of his emotions? Apparently, one day he came home from work tired and exhausted. He simply lost control of his temper for he was in no mood to deal with his ill tempered child. Taking a firm hold of her shoulders, he raised his voice to her and said, "I will not tolerate your tantrums. You are a terrible tempered child". Now his youngest child would carry a heavy burden of shame. Having been labeled by her earthy father as a difficult and unruly child, she was deeply wounded in her spirit. For many years, she would often remember this incident and continue to grieve over it, holding onto a toxic root of bitterness toward her father. Rather than forgiving her father and move on with her new life in Christ, deep resentments would cause frequent eruptions of rage. Now, she not only feared rejection by her earthly father, but dreaded facing further punishment from God. Furthermore, she had a misconception of the Father as an angry God who was quick to judge and punish people. Therefore, she did not open her heart to God not knowing that His heart toward her was full of compassion. She was not aware that His perfect love casts out fear, for fear was the main cause of her anger. Would God deliver her from a spirit of anger and bitterness? She heard within her heart a small Voice that said, "If you are willing to surrender your life to Me, My Spirit of Grace and Truth will set you free." How would God deal with her anger? What does the Bible say about anger?

In His Sermon on the Mount, Jesus equated uncontrolled anger with the spirit of murder.

> You have heard that it was said of old, You shall not murder, and whoever murders will be in danger of judgment. But I say unto you that whoever is angry

with his brother without a cause shall be in danger
of the judgment.   Matthew 5:21, 22

Upon reading this passage in Matthew, she realized that she
must learn how to control her anger or face unpleasant consequences.
The Spirit of the Lord began to challenge her to overcome a root of
bitterness before it would ruin her life and the lives of those around
her. Bitterness caused her to exhibit shameful behavior. Now in the
book of Genesis, the Spirit of the Lord recorded the story about Cain
and Abel for her admonition.

In Genesis chapter four, the tragedy of the first murder is
recorded. Cain, the first born son of Chava and Adam, was a tiller of
the ground and his brother, Abel was a keeper of sheep. "And in the
process of time, it came to pass that Cain brought an offering of the
fruit of the ground to the Lord" (Verse 3). "Abel also brought of the
firstborn of his flock and of their fat. And the Lord respected Abel
and his offering. But He did not respect Cain and his offering. And
Cain was very angry, and his countenance fell" (Verse 4, 5). What
caused the Lord to reject Cain and his offering? One explanation for
his rejection by the Lord was a poor attitude. However, the writer of
Hebrews sheds light on His acceptance of Abel's offering as a more
excellent sacrifice.

"By faith Abel offered to God a more excellent sacrifice than
Cain through which he obtained witness that he was righteous, God
testifying of his gifts; and through it he being dead still speaks".
(Hebrews 11:4)

What did the writer of Hebrews mean by "a more excellent
sacrifice?" To give an answer to this question, remember what the
Lord God did to cover nakedness and shame of Adam and Chava
who ate the "forbidden fruit". In His redemptive plan, He established
the blood sacrifice as the only acceptable offering for sin. In order
to provide adequate clothing as a covering for their nakedness and
shame, the Lord God shed the blood of an innocent animal (Genesis
3:21). Through offering a blood sacrifice, Abel was looking to the

Lord to provide a covering for his sin and to obtain righteousness in His sight. (Hebrews 11:4) By faith, he offered the firstborn of his flock, trusting in the Lord for his salvation, in his expectation of the coming Messiah. As the Lamb of God, the Son of God would offer Himself as the only acceptable Blood sacrifice to fully redeem humanity.

The motive of Cain's offering was to please God with his good works. Through his grain offering, he was attempting to gain favor with the Lord. However, it was in vain, for Cain could not earn his salvation. No man is able to save himself by his good works. "For by grace you have been saved through faith, and that not of yourselves; it is a gift of God, and not of works, lest anyone should boast" Ephesians 2:8, 9). Therefore, the offering of the fruit of the ground was unacceptable sacrifice in the eyes of the Lord. He would only be accepted with the offering of a blood sacrifice because it foreshadows the substitutionary death of Christ on the cross for the redemption of humanity. Therefore, the Lord confronted Cain saying, "If you do well, will you not be accepted? And if you do not do well, sin lies at the door. And its desire is for you, but you should rule over it" (Verse 7). Now, Cain had the opportunity to do what was right in the sight of the Lord, repent and turn away from sin. The Lord expected Cain to take control of his emotions, and rule over them! Like a demon crouching at the door of his heart ready to attack him, hatred and bitterness ruled over his spirit. Nevertheless, Cain failed to obey the Voice of the Lord and repent from his sin of anger toward his brother Abel. Burning with seething rage and bitterness, Cain rose up and murdered him out in a field.

Immediately, the Lord approached Cain asking "Where is Abel your brother?" His response to the Lord was to cover up his sin and lie, taking no responsibility for his actions, "I do not know. Am I my brother's keeper?" (Verse 10). Holding him accountable for the murder of his brother, God required him to make a confession, "What have you done? The voice of your brother's blood cries out to Me from the ground." Failing to confess the sin of murder, Cain faced the judgment of God. For shedding the innocent blood of his brother Abel, the Lord declared that Cain was "cursed from the earth". (*,arar* Strong's# 779, Hebrew verb denoting curse of judgment). "The earth opened its mouth to receive your brother's blood from your hand" (Verse 11). Now, because the blood of his brother was poured out upon the earth, the ground would no longer yield nor produce crops for him. Moreover, he would roam as fugitive and a vagabond upon the earth. As punishment for slaying his brother Abel, the Lord God drove him away from His Presence. In response, Cain cried out, "My punishment is greater than I can bear. Surely, You have driven me out this day from the face of the ground; I shall be hidden from Your face; I shall be a fugitive and a vagabond on the earth, and it will happen that anyone who finds me will kill me" (Genesis 4:14). Now, Cain would be cursed as a wanderer without a place of refuge and a fugitive, fleeing for his life, having been cast away from the Presence of God. However, in His divine mercy, God extended His protection over Cain, placing a mark on him. For he would live in a corrupt society filled with hate, and violence. Woe unto the wicked that are driven by Satan, ruled by a spirit of anger that causes the destruction of human life. Listen to the admonishment of the preacher (*qohelet*) from Ecclesiastes 11:9, 10:

> Rejoice, O young man, in your youth. And let your heart cheer you in the day of your youth; Walk in the ways of your heart, and in the sight of your eyes; But know that for all these God will bring judgment. Therefore remove sorrow from your heart, and put away evil from your flesh, For childhood and youth are vanity.

As all parents recognize in upbringing of their children, they do not have to teach them to sin. All human beings are conceived in sin with a self- centered inclination to disobey the instruction and counsel of their parents. "Behold, I was brought forth in iniquity and in sin, my mother conceived me" (Psalm 51:5). Due to their sin nature, they have a tendency to rebel against authority. Moreover, as they enter into adolescence, young people often succumb to the pressure of their peers. At this time in their life, they are emotionally immature, undergoing hormonal and physical changes and searching for their true identity. "Who am I"? Moreover, they battle insecurity, confusion, and negative feelings toward themselves and others. Furthermore, they cause constant tension at home and at school. Thus, the teen years are filled with turmoil and stress for children and their parents who worry about their future Will they ever grow up to become mature adults as they enter into the real world? As an anxious father, Mr. Brown was worried about the behavior of his youngest daughter.

Kathleen, as a rebellious teenager, struggled with a spirit of anger and hostility toward her father. He attempted to repeatedly warn her to take control of her temper or face the unpleasant consequences of living a life of misery and loneliness. But how does one take control one's emotions? She desperately needed to find answers. While attending Shiloh Bible College, Kathleen began to study the Bible and felt the Spirit of God convicting her of a rebellious attitude. The Spirit revealed that her negative attitude was a major stronghold, holding her back from obtaining victory. Furthermore, it was a heavy weight that hindered her in the race that Christ had set before her. When she read the story about Cain, she realized that she needed to repent and turn to Him for deliverance and salvation. Now, her heavenly Father was waiting to forgive and deliver her from a spirit of bitterness. Throughout her entire lifetime, Father God was extending His grace, and was ready to receive her with His open arms. "The Eternal God is your refuge, and underneath are the everlasting arms" (Deut. 33:27). Gradually, she began to recognize His heart of love and compassion toward her, and His promise to never leave or forsake her. At the same time, as her heavenly Father, He would discipline her. Whenever she lost control of her temper, and lashed out in anger at others, He would utilize His scissors as an instrument of chastisement and trim off the sharp tip of her tongue. Immediately, He would comfort her with His healing words of assurance. Moreover, the indwelling Spirit of God was empowering her to become mature Christian woman. As she learned to respond with humility to His discipline, she was delivered from a stronghold of anger that was preventing her from enjoying an abundant life of joy and happiness. Over many years, Father God was teaching her to show respect towards His authority. In obedience and submission to His Lordship, she gradually began to experience true joy and happiness. As a result of her genuine walk with the Lord, many people observed a gradual transformation of her character and nature. In His Presence, the fruit of the Spirit was being cultivated. Love and compassion replaced bitterness and anger. With an attitude of praise and worship, she became more and more conformed into the image of Christ. She was determined to press on toward her high calling of God in Christ. Empowered by the Holy Spirit, she was able to take more and more control of her spirit. Being led by the Spirit of God, Kathleen no longer fell under the spirit of condemnation. Through cooperation with His Spirit, she renounced a carnal mindset to follow Jesus on the path of eternal life.

Sadly, she saw her former High School friends taking drugs, heading down the road of death and destruction. At the end of the Sermon on the Mount, Jesus told His disciples to enter by the narrow gate, "for wide is the gate and broad is the way that leads to destruction, and there are many who go by it. Because narrow is the gate and difficult is the way which leads to life and there are few who find it" (Matthew 7:13, 14). At one time, many young people had had a relationship with God, but like Cain, they wandered farther and farther away from His Presence. But there was always hope for deliverance and salvation. For the Spirit of the Lord is pouring out His Grace upon this lost generation and drawing them into the Kingdom of God. Now, many young Christians are praying for revival in America and in all the nations of the world!

The Ungodly Seed of Cain

> Cain went out from the presence of the Lord and
> dwelt in the land of Nod in the east of Eden. And
> Cain knew his wife and she bore Enoch. And he
> built a city and called the name of the city after the
> name of his son-Enoch. And he built a city, and
> called the name of the city after the name of his
> son—Enoch. Genesis 4:16, 17.

After Cain left the Presence of the Lord, he dwelt in the land of Nod
(*Nuwd* Strong's # 5110 a Hebrew verb that denotes moving to and
fro, to wander aimlessly as a fugitive, take flight, shake, be disturbed,
agitated, and show grief). He became a fugitive, and an orphan who
no longer lived in the presence of Father God. For Cain, life had no
definite purpose, direction, or meaning. All that he would attempt
to accomplish in his tragic life would be in vain, a chasing after the
wind. Moreover, he would build for himself a corrupt civilization
that had no knowledge of God.

And Cain knew his wife (*yada* Strong's # 3045 Hebrew verb
to know carnally, sexual intercourse). She bore a son Enoch. Cain
built a city that he named and dedicated it after his son, Enoch.
(*Chanowk*. Strong's # 2585 from 2596 *chanak* Hebrew verb to initiate
or discipline—dedicate, train up). Instead of training up his son in
the fear and admonition of the Lord, Cain brought forth an ungodly
seed that became increasingly hostile toward the Lord God and His
Kingdom of righteousness. Living life independently of God, men
drew farther and farther away from His divine plan and purpose
for humanity. Cain and his descendents would no longer worship
or acknowledge the Lord God as their Creator. Instead, men were
hostile toward the Holy One who was their provider and protector.
Now, they began to build a new civilization and a society that would
exalt a name for themselves and their children.

The Genesis of the family of Cain

To Enoch was born Irad; and Irad begot Mehujael,
and Mehujael begot Methushael And Methushael
begot Lamech. Then Lamech took for himself two
wives: the name of one was Adah, and the name of
the second was Zillah. And Adah bore Jabal. He
was the father of those who dwell in tents and have
livestock. His brother's name was Jubal. He was the
father of all those who play the harp and flute. And
as for Zillah, she bore Tubal-Cain, an instructor of
every craftsman in bronze and iron. And the sister
of Tubal-Cain was Naamah. Then Lamech said
to His wives: " Adah and Zillah, hear my voice:...
For I have killed a man for wounding me, even a
young man for hurting me. If Cain shall be avenged
sevenfold, then Lamech seventy-sevenfold.

Genesis 4:18-24.

Genesis 4: 18-24 is an accurate written and historical account of
the genealogy of Cain focusing on the dramatic increase in human
depravity as evil men boasted of their acts of violence and murder.
This biblical narrative portrays the wicked heart of Lamech who
declared to his wives that he killed a young man who had wounded
him. In a spirit of pride, he compared the avengement for his act of
murder to be far greater than that of his forefather Cain. Whereas
Cain was avenged sevenfold for the murder of Abel, Lamech would
be avenged seventy-sevenfold. More and more, the fullness of
vengeance for murder became the norm in a fallen society.

In spite of their spiritual depravity, fallen man's natural skills and
creativity flourished as men were able to establish great cities, develop
various trades and occupations, cultivate the fine arts, and invent

Kathleen Martinez

new rapidly advancing technologies: Jabal was known as the father of tent dwellers and keepers of livestock. As the father of music, Jubal created and designed the harp and the flute. Tubal-Cain instructed his children in the art of crafting bronze and iron. Although the image and likeness of God their Creator was deeply marred, He placed knowledge of His existence in the hearts of humanity. All men were created to be worshippers of God as their Creator with a sense of eternity, a moral conscience, and an awareness of angels as divine beings watching over them.

Seth, the Son of Adam, appointed to be in the bloodline of the Messiah (Luke 3:38)

"And Adam knew his wife again, and she bore a son and named him Seth (*Shet*), For God has appointed another seed for me instead of Abel whom Cain killed." (*shiyth* Strong's # 7896 Hebrew verb that denotes to appoint, array, bring, consider, lay up). In the womb of Chava, God planted the "first son to be in the bloodline" of the Messiah, fulfilling His promise in Genesis 3:15.[43] The one, who had been deceived by Satan, was appointed by God to be the first woman to bear the Seed of the Messianic line. When Chava bore another son to replace Abel, the Lord God was extending His grace and unmerited favor to her and to all humanity. At the time when Enosh, the son of Seth was born, "men began to call on the Name of the Lord" (Genesis 4:26). Living in the midst of darkness, men became desperate for deliverance and began to call on the Name of the Lord with a sincere desire to know Him. As the Spirit of grace drew them, men found a renewed hope in the coming of the Messiah and in His promise of redemption.

---

[43] Jack Hayford Executive Ed, *New Spirit-Filled Life Bible.* (Nashville, TN: Thomas Nelson Publishers, 2002), 11-12.

Genealogy Book of Adam -Seth -Messianic Seed (Genesis 5) [44]

> This is the book (written account) (*cepher* Strong's # 5612 Hebrew noun denotes missive, document, writing) of the genealogy of Adam. In the day that God created man, He made him in the likeness of God. And He created them male and female and blessed them and called them Mankind in the day they were created   Genesis 5:1, 2.

Did Genesis 1-11 originate from oral tradition or from written accounts? According to the text, the reliable sources of Genesis were written accounts, generations, or histories (*toledot*. Strong's #8435 a Hebrew noun denotes history-birth, generations related to the Hebrew verb *yalad* Strong's # 3205 to bear, bring forth, beget). Moses, the author of Genesis, referred to written accounts about real historical people and events. Verified by modern science, the creation of the heavens and the earth is recorded in Genesis 2:4. Genesis 5 is the written genealogical account of the family of Adam. The genealogy of Noah is recorded in Genesis 6:9. Genesis 10:1 provides the written generational line of Shem, Ham and Japheth. The history of Shem is written in Genesis 11:10. The family tree of Terah is recorded in Genesis 11:27.

Therefore, Genesis, as the book of beginnings written in narrative form, focuses on the individual and the family to reveal God's redemptive plan. His plan of redemption was to bring deliverance to all nations through faithful men and their families. Historical and political events of nations do not determine the direction of

---

[44] Walter C. Kaiser, *The Old Testament Documents: Are They Reliable and Relevant?* (Downers Grove, Illinois: InterVarsity Press, 2001), 57-59.

world history, for God is in complete control of all nations as seen in the vision of King Nebuchadnezzar. This vision in Daniel 2: 44, 45 revealed that the history of the world ends with the Kingdom of God. " the God of heaven will set up a kingdom which shall never be destroyed... the stone was cut out of the mountain without hands that broke in pieces the iron, the bronze, the clay, the silver, and the gold – the Great God has made known to the king what will come to pass". While all historical empires eventually fell, the Kingdom of God would never be destroyed, but will stand forever. Hallelujah!

Today, He is calling upon individuals to be instrumental in His redemptive plan. When men and women step out in faith to respond to the call of God, they transform nations and change the course of history. Through the power of the Holy Spirit, they demonstrate the intervention of Kingdom of God in this world with signs, miracles, and wonders. How does humanity know that God is actively involved in the daily life here on earth? Men want to see evidence of His Presence.

"And my speech and my preaching were not with persuasive words of human wisdom, but in demonstration of the Spirit and power, that your faith should not be in the wisdom of men but in the power of God" (I Corinthians 2:4, 5). The lives of men are impacted by the power of the Spirit of God as He moves through His people in the ministries of healing, deliverance, and acts of love, compassion, and kindness. Moreover, the Spirit of God speaks life through His prophetic word of edification, exhortation, and comfort so that people know that God cares for them. He hears their cry for His unconditional love and acceptance. Today, He is Immanuel, God with us. Now, He is revealing His plan of salvation and deliverance. When Christians hear and obey His Voice, they fulfill their calling, and transform the lives of people in their immediate sphere of influence, creating an environment in which God is glorified and magnified. Taking dominion over the kingdom of Satan, the saints of God rule over a world plagued with murder, hate, and violence. Finally, they will rule with Christ forever in His Kingdom!

The Rapid Decline in the Average Lifespan[45]

Before the Fall of Adam, God had created humanity to live forever in a state of perfect harmony and fellowship with Him to be His sons and co-rulers. Through disobedience of one man, sin entered into the world and severed the vital connection of life between humanity and God, causing eternal death and a permanent separation from Him. "Behold, all souls are Mine....For the soul that sins shall die" (Ezekiel 18:4). In Genesis 2:17, the Lord God commanded the man whom He had placed in His garden, not to eat from the tree of the knowledge of good and evil "for in the day that you eat of it, you shall surely die". However, in the day when Adam ate the forbidden fruit, he did not perish immediately within twenty- four hours, but lived within a long extensive period of about one thousand years. According to Moses who wrote Psalm 90:4, a thousand years in the sight of God, "are like yesterday when it is past and like a watch in the night."

Moreover, over the millennia of human history, the life span of mankind significantly declined due to a dramatic increase of the curse brought about by sin, violence, and various environmental factors. During the antediluvian period, the genealogy of Adam recorded that the longevity of human life extended up to nearly one thousand years and then steadily decreased: The days of Methuselah were 969 years. Jared lived up to the age of 962. Noah dwelt on earth for 950 years. The life span of Adam was 930 years. Seth attained the ripe old age of 912 years. Cainan died at the age of 910 years. Enosh inhabited the earth for 905 years. The life of Mahalalel extended up to the age of 895 years.

---

[45] Walter C. Kaiser, *The Old Testament Documents: Are They Reliable and Relevant?* (Downers Grove, Illinois: InterVarsity Press, 2001), 71- 75.

Kathleen Martinez

Moreover, a man of great renown is mentioned by the writer of Hebrews for his remarkable life of faith before God. For only 365 years, Enoch walked with God and was translated, never seeing death. (Genesis 5:23, 24) The Word of God extols Enoch for being one of the outstanding heroes of faith. Throughout his life, Enoch remained steadfast in his relationship with the Lord God while living in a wicked and corrupt generation. Therefore, he had this testimony that he pleased God. (Hebrews 11:5) Today, Christians, who are filled with the Holy Spirit, have the power to live a long life of holiness in a perverse generation that denies the existence of God (Romans 1:18-32)[46] Now, the saints of God live in the last days right before the Second Coming of Christ (Matthew 24:37). The last days are like the days of Noah. What events were transpiring in the days of Noah in Genesis?

---

[46] Hugh Ross. *The Genesis Question: Scientific Advances and the Accuracy of Genesis* (Colorado Springs, Colorado: Navpress Publishing Group, 1998), 118-122,136.

Noahic Flood
The Divine Judgment of Satanic Seed – Preservation of Messianic Seed

Blessed is the man who walks not in the counsel of the ungodly, nor stands in the path of sinners, nor sits in the seat of the scornful. But his delight is in the law of the Lord. And in His law he meditates day and night. He shall be *like a tree* planted by the rivers of water that *brings forth its fruit* in its season, whose leaf also shall not wither; and whatever he does shall prosper. Psalm One

The Spirit of the Lord is upon Me, because the Lord has anointed Me to preach good tidings to the poor. He has sent me to heal the broken hearted, to proclaim liberty to the captives, and the opening of the prison to those who are bound; to proclaim the acceptable year of the Lord, and the day of vengeance of our God; to comfort all who mourn, to console those who mourn in Zion, to give them beauty for ashes, the oil of joy for mourning, the garment of praise for the spirit of heaviness; that they may be called *trees of righteousness,* the planting of the Lord that He may be glorified.Isaiah 61:1-3.

Either make the *tree* good and its *fruit* good, or else make the tree bad and its fruit bad; for a tree is known by its fruit. Matthew 12:33.

A garden enclosed is my sister, my spouse, a spring shut up, a fountain sealed. Awake O north wind, and come O south! Blow upon *my garden* that its spices may flow out. Let my beloved come to *his garden* and eat its pleasant *fruits.*

4:12, 16. Song of Solomon

Now it came to pass, when men began to multiply on the face of the earth, and daughters were born to them, that the sons of God saw that they were beautiful; and they took wives for themselves of all whom they chose.

And the Lord said, "My Spirit shall not strive with men forever, for he is indeed flesh; yet his days shall be one hundred and twenty years... Then the Lord saw that the wickedness of man was great in the earth, and that every intent of the thoughts of his heart was only evil continually. And the Lord was sorry that He had made man on earth, and He was grieved in His heart. So the Lord said," I will destroy man whom I have created from the face of the earth, man and beast, creeping thing and the birds of the air, for I am sorry that I made them.

Genesis 6:1-3, 5-7.

As the population of humanity began to rapidly increase on the face of the earth, men became exceedingly wicked. For their minds were continually filled with thoughts of evil. How did men become so wicked and corrupt after Adam and Eve had been expelled from the Garden of Eden? What really happened in the Garden of Eden? What is the true meaning of the forbidden fruit that sprang forth from the Tree of the Knowledge of Good and Evil? How does one interpret the meaning of the forbidden fruit and the trees in the Garden of Eden? Perhaps, they may be interpreted as symbols that signify a deeper meaning that unlocks a fuller understanding of the original sin of Adam. The nature of his rebellion was a sinister act that caused wide-spread defilement of all flesh. The severity of man's wickedness so grieved the heart of God that He was compelled to declare His judgment saying, "I will destroy man whom I have created from the face of the earth, man and beast, creeping thing, and the birds of the air, for I am sorry that I have made them" (Genesis 6:7). The degree of depravity of all flesh was so heinous in the sight of the Lord that He would undertake drastic measures to wipe all living creatures off the face of the earth.

Moreover, God had to obstruct the evil forces of Satan who sought to destroy the Messianic Seed of the woman (Genesis 3:15). In the fullness of time, the Father would fulfill His promise to send His Beloved Son, the Messiah, who would deliver humanity from the power of Satan' s oppressive kingdom, the overwhelming presence of sin, and the inescapable punishment of death. For death would be an eternal separation from God with no hope of reconciliation. The Son of God, conceived of the Holy Spirit in the womb of a virgin, would come into the darkness of a lost world as a sinless Man to defeat His adversary Satan and to restore a harmonious relationship between humanity and God the Father (Matthew 1:18).

Throughout history, Satan would strive to impede the incarnation of the Messiah knowing that He would come to destroy of his kingdom. As Satan would bruise the heel of Christ through His crucifixion, he would unwittingly cause the destruction of his own kingdom. Through His death on the cross, Jesus won the victory over Satan His adversary and rendered him powerless to afflict humanity with eternal death. Through His resurrection, Christ removed the sting of death so that it would no longer reign over humanity (Genesis 3:15).

Nevertheless, the old serpent, who was Satan himself, had devised a plan to counterfeit the conception of Christ. By what means would he accomplish his wicked plan? Was the forbidden fruit a symbol of sexual perversion that would produce in humanity a corrupt seed planted by Satan? Through the use of His parables as earthly illustrations, Jesus revealed a constant and unrelenting warfare between the Kingdom of God and the kingdom of Satan. In the field of the world, two seeds were being planted in the hearts of men. In the parable of the Wheat and the Tares, He taught that "while men slept, his enemy came and sowed tares among the wheat and went his way. But when the grain had sprouted and produced a crop, then the tares appeared" (Matthew 13:24-26). In the Garden of Eden, Satan planted a seed of corruption in the hearts of Adam and Eve. Is it possible that Satan enticed them to abuse God's gift of sexuality? For He designed humanity to be male and female as sexual partners bound together under the sacred covenant of marriage to be fruitful, multiply, and fill the earth. They were created to be representatives of His Kingdom and His rule on earth. (Genesis 1:26, 27). In the Garden of Eden, marriage between a man and a woman as sexual partners was God's design for procreation. In Song of Solomon, the Spirit of God celebrates the beauty of marital sexuality portrayed as a garden enclosed. The fruit of sexuality is a sacred act that is only performed by a man in an intimate relationship with his beloved spouse. She is his private garden with whom he finds his own pleasures. He is the sole partaker of the pleasant fruits of his garden. No one else can have access to it. No other man may enter into it.

> A garden enclosed is my sister, my spouse, a spring shut up, a fountain sealed. Awake O north wind, and come O south! Blow upon *my garden* that its spices may flow out. Let my beloved come to *his garden* and eat its pleasant *fruits*.
>
> 4:12, 16. Song of Solomon

Moreover, in the original Garden of Eden, God planted trees that were filled with a potential to produce good fruit that was pleasant in the eyes of God and man. According to Isaiah, the trees of God's garden symbolize His people. He created them to be trees of righteousness. They are the planting of the Lord.

> The Spirit of the Lord is upon Me, because the Lord has anointed Me to preach good tidings to the poor. He has sent me to heal the broken hearted, to proclaim liberty to the captives, and the opening of the prison to those who are bound; to proclaim the acceptable year of the Lord, and the day of vengeance of our God; to comfort all who mourn, to console those who mourn in Zion, to give them beauty for ashes, the oil of joy for mourning, the garment of praise for the spirit of heaviness; that they may be called *trees of righteousness,* the planting of the Lord that He may be glorified. Isaiah 61:1-3.

The overall purpose of creating humanity was to give glory to God through good works. God planted His trees to bear the fruit of righteousness. Moreover, the Source of their fruit is the Holy Spirit: But the fruit of the Spirit is love, joy, peace, longsuffering, kindness, goodness, faithfulness, gentleness, self-control. Against such there is no law (Galatians 5:22).

The fruit may only be produced by the Spirit of God as His people abide and remain in His presence and take delight in His Word meditating upon it day and night:

> Blessed is the man who walks not in the counsel of the ungodly, nor stands in the path of sinners, nor sits in the seat of the scornful. But his delight is in the law of the Lord. And in His law he meditates day and night. He shall be *like a tree* planted by the rivers of water that *brings forth its fruit* in its season, whose leaf also shall not wither; and whatever he does shall prosper. Psalm One

Kathleen Martinez

Through meditation and the application of the Word to his personal life, a godly man matures and grows into a fertile tree planted by the rivers of water (the Word of God) that causes him to bring forth fruit in its season. In good times and in bad, his leaf produces healing to the nations. Whatever he does, he prospers. In stark contrast to the righteous, the wicked man produces bad fruit that is the works of the flesh. In his letter to the Galatians, Paul exhorts them to turn away from wickedness:

> Adultery, fornication, uncleanness, lewdness, idolatry, sorcery, hatred, contentions,
> Jealousies, outbursts of wrath, selfish ambitions, dissensions, heresies, envy,
> Murders, drunkenness, revelries and the like; of which I tell you beforehand
> Just as I told you in time past, that those who practice such things will not
> Inherit the Kingdom of God   Galatians 5:20, 21.

As in the days of Noah, the works of the flesh are now in full operation in a fallen, depraved society. Today, the Spirit of the Lord is grieving over the prevailing wickedness of humanity. In order to be true to His holiness, the Lord God must execute His judgments upon the wicked. However, through His divine love and mercy, He exercises forbearance, hoping that His people will repent and turn back to Him so that His judgment can be averted.

> If My people who are called by My Name will humble themselves and pray and seek My face and turn from their wicked ways, then I will hear from heaven, and will forgive their sin and heal their land
> II Chronicles 7:14.

Moreover, His people are admonished by the Spirit to actively pursue godliness and righteousness before the day of their visitation comes to an end.

> Seek the Lord while He may be found. Call upon Him while He is near. Let the wicked forsake his way and the unrighteous man his thoughts; Let him return unto the Lord and He will have mercy on him. And to our God, for He will abundantly pardon   Isaiah 55:6.

Unfortunately, many people refuse to take heed to God's call for repentance while the door of opportunity to receive salvation remains open. Because the day of visitation will soon come to a close, His people must quickly respond to the call of the Spirit and repent now before it is too late. Through receiving the deliverance of God by faith, they may escape the corruption of the world that began in the Garden of Eden.

Kathleen Martinez

The Contentious Debate over the Nature of the Fall of Adam and Eve

In his book, *God's and Thrones: Nachash, Forgotten Prophecy, & the Return of the Elohim,* Carl Gallups refers to several scholarly commentaries that raise some controversial issues concerning the Fall of Adam and Eve. In the twelve -volume *Jewish Encyclopedia,* there is a section titled "Views of the Rabbis." In this commentary, Hebrew scholars make a questionable statement:

> Through the illicit intercourse of Eve with the serpent, however, the nature of her descendents was corrupted, Israel alone overcoming this fatal defect by accepting the Torah at Sinai. [47]

Many modern scholars reject the assertion that Eve entered into an illicit sexual relationship with the serpent that is the symbol of the spirit of Satan who deceived her. "So the great dragon was cast out, that serpent of old, called Devil and Satan who deceives the whole world" (Revelation 12:9). Furthermore, all of her descendents would be defiled by her initial act of sexual perversion. Nevertheless, some Jewish scholars have claimed that through the observation of the Torah, Israel could overcome the original sin of fornication. However, after her deliverance from Egyptian slavery by the almighty Hand of God, Israel rebelled in the wilderness, defiling herself with 'the idols of Egypt'. Sadly, the children of Israel turned away from the Lord God, entering into idol worship, and thus profaning His Name before the nations (Ezekiel 20). At Mount Sinai, the Lord had chosen the children of Israel to be His special people (Exodus

---

[47] Carl Gallups, *God's & Thrones: Nachash, Forgotten Prophecy & the Return of the Elohim* (Crane MO: Defender Publishing, 2017), 185-187,188.

19:6) and gave them His statutes to be a holy kingdom of priests. After He revealed to them His judgments and righteousness, they despised them and refused to observe His statutes and His Sabbaths. Although the first generation had experienced the signs, miracles and wonders of God against Pharaoh and his army, they failed to take hold of His promise to grant them victory over their enemies in Canaan. Therefore, because of their unbelief, the Lord was not able to bring them into the land flowing with milk and honey.

After the Lord brought the next generation into the land of Canaan, the children of Israel defiled themselves following the example of their parents. They provoked the Lord to anger serving idols and profaning His Name (Ezekiel 20:39). Because they continually broke the Mosaic covenant of Mount Sinai, the Lord God ultimately scattered his people throughout the nations of the world. Nevertheless, the Lord had given His people a message of hope while they lived in exile. Now, the Lord is looking forward to the day when Israel will repent as a nation. On that day, He will rejoice over her with great joy and gladness. As the Good Shepherd, the Lord will gather His people out of all the nations of the earth (Ezekiel 34). Upon returning to the land of Israel, they will hallow His great Name, walking in obedience to His commandments. Through His faithful people, He will be sanctified and set apart from all gods. When the children of Israel fear and exalt His Name, the nations will know that He is the Lord. Moreover, He will purify them with the water of His Word, cleansing them from their filthiness and idolatry. He will give them a new heart of flesh that will love and obey Him. He will put a new spirit within them. His indwelling Spirit will cause them to walk in His statutes and keep His judgments so that they may dwell forever in the land (Ezekiel 36:16-38).

Another commentary *New World Encyclopedia* makes a similar assertion that Eve entered into a sexual intercourse with Satan in an entry "Human Fall":

Some early Christian sects and rabbinical sages considered that the Fall was the result of sexual intercourse between Eve and the Serpent, usually understood to symbolize Satan... Christianity traditionally teaches that Original Sin is passed on through sexual intercourse, interpreting Psalm 51:5, "I was brought forth in iniquity, and in sin did my mother conceive me" [48]

In heaven, the spirit of rebellion originally began with Satan and his fallen angels (Ezekiel 28:15). Satan, the covering cherub over the throne of God, profaned himself. Therefore, God removed him from his exalted position in His Holy Mountain. According to Ezekiel 28:16, God cast Satan as a *profane* thing out of heaven:

Therefore, I cast you as a profane thing out of the Mountain of God; And I Destroyed you, O covering cherub, from the midst of the fiery stones.

(Profane #2490 Strong's *chalal denotes pollute, defile, profane or prostitute one self sexually* Niphal stem.)

The sin of prostitution, practiced in the Near East, was an abomination in the sight of God. He brought immediate retribution upon those who would defile or pollute themselves through fornication. In ancient Israel, women who prostituted themselves were severely punished :

Leviticus 21:9 "The daughter of any priest, if she profanes herself by playing the harlot, she profanes her father. She shall be burned with fire."

[48] Carl Gallups, *God's & Thrones: Nachash, Forgotten Prophecy & the Return of the Elohim* (Crane MO: Defender Publishing, 2017), 185-187,188.

> Genesis 38: 24 ... Judah was told, saying, "Tamar played the harlot...So Judah said, "Bring her out and let her be burned."

Prostitution in ancient Israel was a grave sin that was punishable by fire. For the sin of fornication, Tamar faced being burned by fire. Due to sexual promiscuity, the men of Sodom and Gomorrah were also destroyed with brimstone and fire (Genesis 19: 24). What causes men and women to commit sexual promiscuity incurring divine judgment of fire? It is a spirit of lust. Ultimately, the wicked will be cast into the Pit, the Lake of Fire along with the sons of God who lusted after the daughters of men. Many scholars continue to debate the identity of the *Bene Elohim* in Genesis 6:1-4? Who were they?

Bene Elohim

According to *Ellicott's Commentary for English Readers*, three explanations of their identity are given: [49] High ranking noble men, divine beings—angels, or the sons of Seth from the line of Cain who was the first murderer.

The Targum and Jewish expositors claim that they were rulers, and high ranking men of society. In the Near East society, *bin il* (son of God) was a title for nobles, aristocrats and kings.[50] The rulers who pursued wealth, power, and fame were free to marry any woman that they desired. They "came into daughters of men and bore children to them." The rich and powerful leaders married women of a lower rank in society and entered into a sociological blended union. Kings, who desired to obtain absolute authority over their subjects, claimed to be titular descendents of the gods. In Egypt, the pharaohs called themselves the "son of Amon", the "son of Re", or the "son of Atum". Through laying hold of the title "sons of the gods", they were granted the right of kingship to rule over the people.

Today, modern scholars are of the opinion that the sons of Seth through the line of Cain lusted after beautiful women. They brought forth "mighty men of renown" who were strong warriors. But how were ordinary mortal men able to procreate a race of men who attained overwhelming stature and possessed supernatural strength? They were violent, belligerent men who threatened to destroy humanity through the invention of deadly weapons, causing warfare that would plague men throughout human history. These mighty warriors were fallen men or *Nephim*. (Strong's # 5309 *nephel* denoting fallen from the Hebrew verb #5307 naphal to fall) The

---

[49] Carl Gallups, *God's & Thrones: Nachash, Forgotten Prophecy & the Return of the Elohim* (Crane MO: Defender Publishing, 2017), 200-201.
[50] Walter C. Kaiser Jr., *The Old Testament Documents; Are They Reliable & Relevant?* (Downers Grove, Illinois: InterVarsity Press, 2001)77-79.

Hebrew word *Nephim* was translated in the Greek Septuagint as *gigantes*. The English translation is "giants" in King James Version. The Greek word *gegenes* denotes Titans who were part terrestrial and part celestial beings that were 'earth-born.' Moreover, *Nephilim* denotes fallen ones as offspring of an unholy marital union. [51] Therefore, Genesis 6:1-4 refers to these men as *Nephilim,* monsters, and terrorists that tormented ordinary men. They provoked great fear in all the nations of the Near East.

As the children of Israel were preparing to go in and take possession of Canaan, they sent out spies to view the land. Unfortunately, when ten of the spies returned, they discouraged the Israelites, delivering a negative report. They were fearful of the men of great stature. In comparison to these giants, the children of Israel appeared in their own eyes to be weak and powerless like grasshoppers. This disturbing account presented by these cowardly, faithless men caused great fear to rise up in the hearts of God's people. In Numbers 13:33, the emotion of fear blinded their eyes so that they were not able to see that their God was an invincible Man of war. As the Almighty God, He was able to conquer and destroy all of their enemies great and small.

Today, fear often grips the hearts of people who hear day after day evil reports from the media. They lack faith to believe God to do great miracles on their behalf. Americans watch in horror the reports of young students who carry guns into schools to massacre innocent children. No one feels safe in schools, at work and other public places. There is a public outcry for security and for stricter laws of gun control. The only solution to ending the wave of violence and hatred is sincere heartfelt repentance in the Church that will bring a renewal of the Christian faith in God to save America. When Christians humble themselves, and turn to the Lord in true repentance, then the Spirit of God will hear their cry for deliverance,

---

[51] C. Fred Dickason, *Revised and Expanded Angels Elect & Evil* (Chicago: Moody Publishers, 1975, 1995) 244,245.

Kathleen Martinez

forgive their sin of hate and self indulgence and heal their land. The Lord will grant them peace and safety. Who were the sons of God who bore the *Nephilim*?

Lately, some scholars claim that the sons of God were divine beings or angels. An in-depth research of the Scriptures unlocks and reveals the true meaning of difficult passages. New Testament writers compare false teachers guilty of sexual perversion with the fallen angels now bound in the Pit, awaiting divine judgment (II Peter 2:4-5 and Jude 6-7).

For if God did not spare the angels who sinned, but cast them into hell (*Tartarus*) And delivered them into chains of darkness to be reserved for judgment and did not spare the ancient world, but saved Noah, one of eight people, a preacher of righteousness, bringing in a flood on the world of the ungodly. And turning the cities of Sodom and Gomorrah into ashes, condemned them to destruction, making them an example to those who afterward would live ungodly...then the Lord knows how to deliver the godly out of temptations and to reserve the unjust under punishment for the day of judgment and especially those who walk according to the flesh in the lust of uncleanness and despise authority. They are presumptuous, self-willed. They are not afraid to speak evil of dignitaries. II Peter 2:4, 5, 9, 10.

In his second epistle, Peter associated false teachers "who walk according to the flesh in the lust of uncleanness" with fallen angels who sinned and were cast into hell reserved for the Day of Judgment." The apostle issued a stern warning to sexual predators, alluding to the Old Testament accounts of the judgments of God. In ancient biblical times, humanity was not spared His judgment. In the days of Noah, God wiped out all corrupted flesh with a universal flood. The sexually perverse cities of Sodom and Gomorrah were reduced to ashes. Fire from heaven fell upon immoral men who lusted after sexual relations with angels. Surely, immoral and depraved teachers who lust after women committing fornication will face the Day of Judgment along with the fallen angels that have been cast into the Pit of Hell. Peter compares such debased men with those who perished in the Noahic flood and in the fire that consumed the cities of Sodom and Gomorrah. How are Christians able to escape the corruption that is in the world today?

Peter exhorts the church to resist temptation by embracing the promises of God

> Grace and peace be multiplied to you in the knowledge of God and of Jesus Our Lord as His divine power has given to us all things that pertain to life and godliness through the knowledge of Him who called us by glory and virtue by which have been given to us exceedingly *great and precious promises* that through these you may be partakers of the divine nature, having escaped the corruption that is in the world through lust.   I Peter 1:2-4

Christians must resist temptation through personal knowledge of Christ as Lord and Savior, along with daily study and application of His Word. God has given His people exceedingly great promises of His power and grace to overcome the lust of the world and be partakers of His divine nature. Christians do not need to yield to the spirit of lust, the original sin that began in the Garden of Eden. Lust (*epithumia* Strong's # 1939 denotes "a longing for what is forbidden—concupiscence a strong desire lust after). [52] A biblical example of godliness and blameless character is Noah, the preacher of righteousness.

---

[52] Carl Gallups, *God's & Thrones: Nachash, Forgotten Prophecy & the Return of the Elohim* (Crane MO: Defender Publishing, 2017), 191,192.

Noah a Preacher of Righteousness

> By faith Noah, being divinely warned of things not yet seen, moved with godly fear, prepared an ark for the saving of his household, by which he condemned the world, and became an heir of the righteousness which is according to faith.
>
> Hebrews 11:7

Noah found favor with God. Because He was a righteous man, blameless among the people of his time; he walked with God. (*Tamiym Strong's 8549* a Hebrew adjective denoting one who is sound, complete, entire, wholesome, innocent, having integrity). Noah, son of Lamech was a God fearing man. Like his ancestor Seth and Enosh, he was a seeker of God's Kingdom and His righteousness (Genesis 4:26). Noah proceeded from the pure, undefiled seed of Seth. Therefore, his name is listed in the genealogy of Jesus Christ (Luke 3:36). Furthermore, his name Noah means "rest" (*Noach* Strong's 5146 from the verb *Nuwach* Strong's #5118 denoting quiet and rest). Lamech called his son Noah saying "This one will comfort us concerning our work and the toil of our hands because of the ground which the Lord has cursed" (Genesis 5:29).

Noah took heed to the Word of God, warning him of His upcoming judgment upon all flesh, "I will destroy them with the earth" (Genesis 6:13). As a man who feared God, he "prepared an ark for the saving of his household". Through his dynamic faith, he was obedient to God. He built an ark for his family and thereby he condemned the world. By faith, Noah became an heir of righteousness in the Kingdom of God.

Moreover, God established His covenant with him and his family. The Lord said to Noah, "Come into the ark, you and your household, because I have seen that you are righteous before Me in this generation" (Genesis 7:1). (*tsaddiyq* Strong's #6662 just, lawful righteous in conduct and character before God). Exhibiting irreproachable conduct and character, Noah was steadfast in his relationship with God. In an atmosphere of intense darkness and wickedness, this man was a beacon of light and a preacher of truth and the fear of God. Unfortunately, his generation failed to respond to God's urgent call for repentance. On the Day of Judgment, the fountains of the great deep were broken up and the windows of heaven were opened. Noah, along with his family had entered into the ark of safety. Moreover, the Lord had brought animals into Noah's ark to preserve them. Then God shut the door for the period of grace, during which the opportunity for the wicked to repent, had transpired. All living things were destroyed from the earth by a universal flood.

Today, as in the days of Noah, the Church is called upon by God to repent before He sends judgment upon America and the world. Many people are too busy with their daily life to take heed to the Voice of God. Therefore, He allows horrific storms of nature and acts of violence to awaken His people. During a period of grace, they may seek Him and turn from their wicked ways. "Seek the Lord while He may be found. Call upon while He is near" (Isaiah 55:6). Furthermore, the Lord always issues warnings before He sends judgment upon His unrepentant people. They are inundated with a flood of lies and deception, living in an immoral society that rejects God and His commandments.

Noahic Covenant

Nevertheless, the Lord has promised humanity that He will never send a universal flood to destroy all flesh. God remembered Noah and every living thing and all the animals that were with him in the ark. After he and his family departed from the ark, Noah built an altar in dedication to the Lord and offered up burnt offerings. The heart of God was pleased and established a covenant with all creatures and future generations of humanity[53].

> "I will never again curse the ground for man's sake, although the imagination of man's heart is evil from his youth, nor will I again destroy every living thing as I have done. While the earth remains, seedtime and harvest, cold and heat, winter and summer, and day and night shall not cease   Genesis 8,21,22.

Although humanity would continue to be controlled by a hostile spirit toward the Lord God, He would not propagate the curse on earth. In His forbearing Spirit, he would continue to bestow His blessings of abundant provision, grace, and mercy toward all living things under His new covenant with Noah, his descendents, and all living creatures on earth. While the earth remained in a fallen state, humanity would continue tilling the soil, sewing seed, and producing a harvest. Moreover, as long as the earth remained, the seasons of winter and summer, day and night would not come to an end. As a sign of His faithfulness to keep His promises, the Lord set His rainbow that would be observed by man and all creatures. The

---

[53] Kevin J. Conner and Ken Malmin, *The Covenants: The Key to God's Relationship with Mankind.* (Portland, Oregon: City Bible Publishing, 1983). 22-26.

rainbow, as a sign of His covenant, would cause Him to remember His promise to all flesh. And He would always be true to His Word.

In order to repopulate the earth, Lord blessed Noah and his sons Shem, Ham, and Japheth, "Be fruitful, and multiply and fill the earth" (Genesis 9:1). The initial command of the Lord God for humanity in Genesis 1:28, 29 continued to be efficacious for men to procreate and fill the entire face of the earth. Moreover, all creatures would be subservient to the rule and care of men (Genesis 2:19, 20). In His covenant with Noah, the Lord God modified the diet of men, permitting them to consume all living creatures. However, they were prohibited from eating flesh with the blood for the life is in the blood (Leviticus 17: 10-16). Furthermore, due to the sacredness of human life, created in the image of God, murder would be a capital crime punishable by death under the authority of the government of men. However, would human leadership be subject to the Kingdom of God or become subservient to the "god of this world"?

The Call of Abraham the Father of the Faithful - Friend of God

"The bricks have fallen down, but we will rebuild with hewn stones" Isaiah 9:10 Pride goes before destruction and a haughty spirit before a fall.
Proverb 16:18

In Genesis 9:1, God reinstated His original plan and purpose for humanity and blessed Noah and his sons. And He said to them, "Be fruitful and multiply and fill the earth." However, in Genesis 11, the descendents of Noah rebelled against His mandate to fill the earth, when they "journeyed from the east to a plain in the land of Shinar." Upon settling there, they set forth a plan to build a magnificent city. How would they build city? What was their true motive for building a tower that would reach up to the heavens? "They said to one another, 'Come, let us make bricks and bake them thoroughly.' They had brick for stone and they had asphalt for mortar" (Genesis 11:3). And they said, "Come, let us build ourselves a city, and a tower, whose top is in the heavens; let us make a name for ourselves, lest we be scattered over the face of the whole earth" (Genesis 11:4). What was their true motive for building a city and a tower that would reach up to the heavens?

In reality, Satan was implementing his own agenda in the minds of wicked men : to ascend up to heaven, to exalt his throne above the stars of God, to sit on the mount of the congregation on the farthest sides of the north, to ascend above the heights of the clouds and to be like the Most High (Isaiah 14:13,14). Throughout history, men have been constructing enormous skyscrapers in attempt to reach up to the heavens and exalt themselves above God. From His throne on high, the Lord has observed men, constructing their cities building their own kingdoms. "The Lord came down to see the city and the tower which the sons of men had built." Through a common language, they were united to "make a name for themselves." In a spirit of pride, they rose up in rebellion against the rule of God to establish a one world government. When the Lord of hosts viewed their tower, He said to His heavenly council, "Come, let Us go down and there confuse their language that they may not understand one another's speech" (Genesis 11:7). Why did the Lord confuse their language? He caused the confusion of their language so that humanity would spread out over the entire face of the earth. Now this was His original plan for humanity on the day He created them. In Genesis 1:27, 28, God blessed male and female on the day He created them in His image and likeness to "be fruitful and multiply and fill the earth." Thus, humanity would exercise dominion on earth as His representatives of His glorious Kingdom. The Light and divine order of the Kingdom of God would stand in victory with absolute power and authority over Satan's kingdom of darkness and confusion. As the Lord scattered men over the face of the earth, they ceased building the city. As a result, the name of the abandoned city was Babel meaning confusion. While He observed the darkness and disorder in the world, the Lord God began to seek a man through whom He would establish His redemptive plan on earth. His desire was to restore His unbroken relationship with humanity made in His image and likeness.

At the end of the primeval period, the descendents of Noah were scattered over the face of the earth, forming new nations with their own unique culture, language, and religion. Genesis 11:10-32 records the genealogy of Shem, marking a significant transition from primeval history into the period of the patriarchs. Furthermore, within nine generations from Noah to Abraham, the life span of humanity was significantly shortened from 950 to 175 years. [54] At

---

[54] Jack W. Hayford, *New Spirit-Filled Life Bible: Kingdom Equipping Through the Power of the Word NKJV.* (Nashville, Tennessee: Thomas Nelson, Inc.,

Kathleen Martinez

this time, the Lord appointed a man of faith through whom He would create a new nation in order to commence His redemptive plan to liberate the world from sin and darkness. Abram was the man who responded to the call of the Lord God to leave his country, travel to a new land of inheritance, and become the father of the faithful?

> By faith, Abraham obeyed when he was called to go out to the place which he would receive as an inheritance. And he went out, not knowing where he was going
>
> Hebrews 11:8.

> And the Lord said to Abram, "Get out of your country, from your family and from your father's house to the land that I will show you"
>
> Genesis 12:1.

What inspired Abram to leave his country Ur of the Chaldees in southwest Mesopotamia to travel northwest up to Haran where he heard the Voice of the Lord calling him to go to a foreign land? [55] What would cause him to depart from a highly civilized center of Mesopotamia known for arts, law, commerce, and travel to a distant land of Canaan? Deep within his heart and mind, Abram rejected paganism, a pantheon of gods who caused darkness and chaos in the world. As the patriarch and head of his own family, Abram left his homeland to separate himself from the idolatry of his father's house. His departure was an act of rebellion against paganism, and the worship of the oppressive forces of nature. As a man of faith, Abram boldly embraced the revelation of the Lord as the one and only true God of the universe. Although he did not know where he was going,

---

2002). 18,19.

[55] Abba Eban, *My People: The Story of the Jews New Edition*. (New York: Behrman House Inc., 1984). 4,5.

he obeyed His Voice, trusting in His goodness. As a benevolent God and loving Father, the Lord declared to Abram His great promises:

> I will make you a great nation; I will bless you and make your name great and you will be a blessing. And I will bless those who bless you. And I will curse him who curses you. And in you all the families of the earth shall be blessed.   Genesis 12: 2, 3.

Abram, through his obedience to the call of God, would become the progenitor of a great nation of kings and priests sanctified and set apart unto Him. He would have His special people who would glorify Him as the Sovereign Lord who reigns over all the nations of the world. Through the nation of Israel, God would reinstate His Kingdom upon earth as it is in heaven. They would be created as devoted worshippers who would love and serve their Lord God. The Lord promised to bless him causing him to be happy and prosperous. (barak, Strongs # 1288, a Hebrew verb, denoting to bless, salute, congratulate, thank, praise, to kneel down). Moreover, his name would be great as a man of faith who dedicated his life to worship God. As Abram served Him in loving obedience, God blessed him with abundant life, fame, and wealth. Furthermore, Abram would be a blessing to all nations for from his loins would come forth the Messiah, the Seed of the woman (Genesis 3:15) who would be the Savior and Redeemer of the world. The Gospel of Matthew commences with an opening title; "The book of the genealogy of Jesus Christ, the Son of David, the Son of Abraham" (Matthew 1:1). Furthermore, in the Gospel of Matthew, the Name of the Savior is recorded. "And she will bring forth a Son, and you shall call His Name Jesus, for He will save His people from their sins" (Matthew 1:21).

Those who bless Abram and his descendents would be blessed with the abundance and fullness of life in the Kingdom of God. By faith, trusting and believing in Christ as their personal Lord and

Savior, they would be born again to enter into the spiritual realm of God's Kingdom. (John 3:5) The process of being born again requires repentance that is a process involving a radical change of heart attitude toward God and a yielding of one's own will to His perfect will. Upon repentance, one is born into the family of God the Father. By faith alone in God's grace and favor, a child of God receives the gift of salvation. According to Paul in Ephesians 2:8, 9, "For by grace, you have been saved through faith, and not of yourselves, it is a gift of God, not of works lest anyone should boast." One is incapable of earning salvation by good works but must rely on the work of Christ who shed His Blood on the cross for his redemption.

In contrast to the blessings of those who bless Abraham is the punishment of those who curse him. They shall incur His divine judgment. ('arar, Strong's # 779, a Hebrew verb denoting execrate, denunciate, declared evil, invoking harm, to curse). An accursed thing or person who rebels against the will of God is devoted to utter destruction as observed in the case of Achan, the troubler of Israel. For his disobedience against God, Achan caused the Lord's wrath to fall upon Israel. He was condemned, and put to death (Joshua 7: 25, 26).

Therefore, anyone who opposes Israel and the Kingdom of God will face the wrath of God on the final Day of Judgment. They will be totally annihilated. At the Great White Throne, all "the dead will be judged according to their works by the things which were written in the books...And anyone not found written in the Book of Life was cast into the lake of fire" (Revelation 20:12, 15). Thus, all who have rejected the gift of His salvation will face the terrible indignation and anger of God and will be cast into the Lake of Fire. In the eternal place of torment, the condemned will be separated from the Lord God forever.

At the age of seventy-five, Abram departed from Haran taking his wife Sarai and Lot, the son of his deceased brother and the people whom he had acquired as slaves. He entered into the land of Canaan.

(Genesis 12:5)[56] Upon hearing the Voice of God, Abram journeyed south, taking a step of faith, not knowing where he was going. "Then the Lord appeared to Abram and said, 'To your descendents I will give this land'" (Genesis 12:7). Upon hearing the Voice of the Lord God, Abram stepped into the Land of his inheritance. Observing his obedience, the Lord appeared to him declaring a promise to his descendents. They would inherit the land of Canaan. As a result of Abram's obedience, the Lord granted him an eternal inheritance. The Promised Land would be the dwelling place of Israel forever. In response to God's promise of land to his children, Abram built an altar in dedication, calling upon the Name of the Lord who appeared to him (Genesis 4:26). The Lord said to Abram, "Lift your eyes now and look, from the place where you are—northward, southward, eastward, and westward, for all the land which you see I give you and your descendents *forever*" (Genesis 13:14,15). Moreover, the descendents of Abram would be numerous. In great numbers, they would even exceed "the dust of the earth".

The blessings of the Lord continued to abound upon Abram. Upon receiving a report of the captivity of Lot, his brother's son, Abram "armed three hundred and eighteen trained servants, born in his own house, and went in pursuit as far as Dan" (Genesis14:14). As a mighty military leader, Abram divided his army at night, attacked his enemies, and drove them north of Damascus. Through his successful military campaign, Abram was able to liberate Lot and deliver men and women of his household. Moreover, Abram brought back the spoils of war, and greatly increased his own wealth.

After Abram achieved resounding victory over Chedorlaomer, King of Elam and his allies, Melchizedek, King of Salem, came out to meet him. He brought him bread and wine.(Genesis 14:18) As priest of God, Most High, he blessed Abram and said, " Blessed be Abram of God Most High, Possessor of heaven and earth; And

---

[56] Jack W. Hayford, *New Spirit-Filled Life Bible: Kingdom Equipping Through the Power of the Word.* (Nashville, Tennessee: Thomas Nelson, Inc., 2002). 21.

Kathleen Martinez

blessed be God Most High Who has delivered your enemies into your hand" (el 'elyon Strong's #5945 Hebrew adjective denoting God, the Most High). At the birth of Christ, angelic host from heaven declared, "Glory to God in the highest, and on earth peace and goodwill toward men" (Luke2:14). [57] The God of Abram who called him out of Ur of Chaldea to inherit the land of Canaan, is the called the Most High, Possessor of heaven and earth. Therefore, The Most High God, the Supreme Ruler of the universe, was able to deliver his enemies into his hand. He drove them out beyond Dan into the far north. Who was Melchizedek? According to the writer of Hebrews, Melchizedek was

> Priest of the Most High God who met Abram …
> and blessed him. He was king of righteousness and
> king of Salem meaning " king of peace" without
> father, without mother, without genealogy, having
> neither beginning of days nor end of life but made
> like the Son of God remains a priest continually
> Hebrews 7:1,3

Melchizedek was the king of righteousness. He was the king of peace who had no record of his genealogy. Moreover, he appears to be like the Son of God, having neither beginning of days nor end of life. Upon receiving the blessings of Melchizedek, Abram gave him a tithe of all his wealth. The giving of the tithe was an act of worship. Abram who was acknowledging that God is the King of Righteousness. By faith, he knew that the Most High God is good. He is faithful to fulfill all of His everlasting promises to His people. According to the Gospel of John, Christ, the Son of God, the Word of God was in the beginning with God (John 1:1; 2). Because Christ is the eternal Son of God who gave His life as a sacrifice to save

---

[57] Jack W. Hayford, *New Spirit-Filled Life Bible: Kingdom Equipping Through the Power of the Word.* (Nashville, Tennessee: Thomas Nelson, Inc., 2002). 23

humanity, His priesthood will continue forever according to the order of Melchizedek (Hebrews 7:17).

After his encounter with Melchizedek, the Word of the Lord came to Abram in a vision, saying, "Do not be afraid, Abram, I am your shield, your exceedingly great reward" (Genesis 15:1). In response to the promise of His divine protection and favor, Abram confronted God about being childless. "Lord God, what will you give me, seeing I go childless and the heir of my house is Eliezer of Damascus?" The word of the Lord came to him, saying, "This one will not be your heir, but one who will come from your own body shall be your heir" (Genesis 15:4). In His set time, Abram and his wife Sarai would conceive and bare a son. "And the Lord visited Sarah as He had said, and the Lord did for Sarah as He had spoken. For Sarah conceived and bore Abraham a son in his old age at the set time of which God had spoken to him" (Genesis 21:1, 2).

Moreover, his descendants would be as innumerable as the stars of heaven. The Lord told Abram to go outside and "look now toward the heaven and count the stars if you are able to number them... So shall your descendants be" (Genesis 15:5). Through their telescopes, modern astronomers of today are not able to count all the stars in His immense universe which stretches beyond human imagination. In response to the Word of the Lord, Abram "believed in the Lord, and He accounted it to him for righteousness" Genesis 15:6). (*Chashab* Strong's #2803 denoting to think, reckon, put together, calculate, imagine, impute, make account). [58] The Lord counted Abram's faith as righteousness. He accredited and reckoned every act of his obedience, creating an account as a record of his righteousness of faith. For Abram was placing his complete trust in His Word believing in all of His promises. Therefore, he is called the father of all who believe.

---

[58] Jack W. Hayford, *New Spirit-Filled Life Bible: Kingdom Equipping Through the Power of the Word*. (Nashville, Tennessee: Thomas Nelson, Inc., 2002). 24

For the promise that he would be the heir of the world was not to Abraham or to his seed through the law, but through righteousness of faith... it is of faith that it might be according to grace so that the promise might be sure to all the seed not only to those who are of the law but also to those who are of faith of Abraham who is the father of us all.

Romans 4:13, 16.

Here, Paul is asserting that Abraham did not obtain righteousness through observing the law or following any legal statutes. He was declared righteous by the Lord God for his faith that he had demonstrated through obedience to His Voice. At the command of the Lord, he had left his family, his homeland, and his culture to follow Him. Although Abram did not fully understand the unfolding of the Lord's plan for his life, he was willing to take steps of faith, trusting in His love, goodness, and divine favor. Moreover, by faith, Abram had developed an intimate relationship with the Lord God. He loved God and fully entrusted his life into His care. He believed the Word of God.

"I am the Lord who brought you out of Ur of the Chaldeans to give you this land to inherit it"

Abram wanted to have absolute confidence in His promise to give him the land of Canaan as inheritance. However, he was childless. To whom would he pass on his inheritance? He inquired of the Lord. Genesis 15:7. Now Abram confronted the Lord for he and his wife were childless saying, "Lord God how shall I know that I will inherit the land?" In response to his inquiry, the Lord God established a sacred blood covenant with Abram and his children. What is a covenant? What would be the eternal significance of the covenant that the Lord created with Abram and his descendents?

The Abrahamic Covenant

A covenant (*beriyth* Strong's #1285 denotes a compact that implies act of cutting) is a bond that binds two or more individuals in a sacred union requiring a steadfast commitment that could not be broken without the grave consequence of death. A biblical covenant was a bond in blood initiated and administered by the Sovereign Lord God with men.[59] The first shedding of blood occurred in the Garden of Eden. Immediately after the Fall of Adam and Eve, the Lord God initiated the shedding of blood of an animal. It was a sacrificial offering that would cover the shame and nakedness of a fallen humanity. Now, Adam and Eve were no longer clothed in the glory of His Presence. Sadly, their disobedience caused a broken relationship with God and with one another. Furthermore, they were under the sentence of death, and would be separated from God forever. The first blood sacrifice foreshadowed the death of His only Son on the cross as a divine work of restoration and deliverance.

Through His covenant with Abram in Genesis 15, the Lord Himself initiated His redemptive work. The essential element in the establishment of this covenant was the shedding of blood. The life of the flesh is in the blood... for it is the blood that makes atonement for the soul (Leviticus 17:11). During this covenant ritual, the blood of animals was shed to demonstrate the solemnity of entering into a covenantal bond. In Genesis 15: 9, 10, He instructed Abram, "bring Me a three year-old heifer, a three year-old female goat, a three year old ram, a turtledove and a young pigeon ... and cut them in two, down the middle and place each piece opposite the other." In a customary traditional ceremony of the near East, Lord God requested Abram to bring the Lord God five animals: a heifer,

---

[59] O. Palmer Robertson, *The Christ of the Covenants* (Phillipsburg, New Jersey: Presbyterian and Reformed Publishing Company, 1980), 4.

Kathleen Martinez

a female goat, and a ram cut in half and placed in two rows opposite of one another. However, the birds were not cut in two.

At night fall, Abram fell into a deep sleep. A great darkness and a deep sense of horror came upon him in a dream; God warned him that his descendants would be afflicted in a foreign land. After four hundred years of slavery in Egypt, they would return to the land of their inheritance. In the darkness of night, a smoking oven and a burning torch appeared passing between the slain animals to signify that God would be faithful to fulfill His promise to Abram and his descendants, taking an oath of loyalty. [60] The Lord Himself passed between the slain carcasses. As an act of humility, God placed Himself in an inferior position to establish the Abrahamic Covenant. Furthermore, God would offer up His only Son to be the Blood sacrifice that would save humanity from sin and death. Therefore, the animal sacrifices of the Abrahamic Covenant foreshadowed substitutionary death of the Lamb of God. Jesus Christ was the Lamb who was slain before the foundation of the world according to Revelation 13:8. As the Good Shepherd, he was willing to lay down His life responding to the command of His Father. (John 10: 17, 18). The Lord Jesus fulfilled original promise of His Father to send forth His Redeemer in Genesis 3:15. The Messiah who is the "Seed of the woman" was willing to die in order to restore eternal life to humanity. Now through the Abrahamic Covenant, His people will be bonded together in an everlasting relationship with God the Father. Thirteen years later, the Lord would reaffirm His covenant with Abram.

---

[60] Jack W. Hayford, *New Spirit-Filled Life Bible: Kingdom Equipping Through the Power of the Word.* (Nashville, Tennessee: Thomas Nelson, Inc., 2002). 25.

The Sign of the Covenant

At the advanced age of ninety-nine, the Lord appeared to Abram and said to him, "I am Almighty God, walk before me and be blameless. I will make my covenant between Me and you and will multiply you exceedingly" (Genesis 17:1, 2). (Almighty *Shadday* Strong's #7706 denotes all powerful One who (*sheh*) is sufficient (*day*) as the all Sufficient One).[61]

Thirteen years after the Lord God made a covenant with Abram, He appears again to him declaring His Name as the Almighty God. He commands Abram to walk before Him and be blameless (*naqiy* Strong's #5355 denoting clean, clear, free, guiltless, innocent) as one who is above reproach. Moreover, the Almighty further clarifies His covenant with Abram, reaffirming His promise to "multiply him exceedingly". Abram, who has been called "exalted father" (*Ab Strong's # 1 rum* Strong's # 7311) will now be known as the father of many nations (*Abraham Strong's #5971 'am* denoting men, nation, and people). As for Sarai, his wife, her new name shall be (*Sarah* Strong's # 8282 princess), a mother of nations. (Genesis 17:15, 16) Abraham and Sarah are greatly blessed and being made exceedingly fruitful, for through them the Lord God would bring forth nations and kings. Furthermore, His covenant with Abraham and Sarah would extend to their descendants as an "everlasting covenant". The Almighty would reaffirm His promise to them and their seed to inherit the land of Canaan as an "everlasting possession" where He will be their God (Genesis 17:8). However, how would His promise of bearing a multitude of descendents come to pass?

How could a man who is one hundred years old and a woman

---

[61] Jack W. Hayford, *New Spirit-Filled Life Bible: Kingdom Equipping Through the Power of the Word.* (Nashville, Tennessee: Thomas Nelson, Inc., 2002). 757

Kathleen Martinez

of ninety years bear a child? A divine calling to bear a child in their old age would require a divine infusion of life from the Spirit of God to quicken their frail bodies. Moreover, this miracle would be signified by a changing of their names. Moreover, the blood covenant would require an exchange of names. Therefore, when God renamed Abram, He added a *"Hei"* to his name. What does *"Hei"* signify? The letter *Hei* in the Hebrew Alphabet represents the breathe of God.[62] He also added the *Hei* to the name of his wife Sarai. From His holy name *YHVH*, God contributed two *Hei*'s or half of His divine Name to affirm His covenant with Abraham and Sarah. Just as the Spirit of God breathed the breath of life into Adam to cause him to become a living being in Genesis 2:7, the breath of the Holy Spirit quickened their antiquated bodies in order to conceive and bear Isaac. Of course, Abraham and Sarah laughed when God, the Almighty, announced that they would have a son in their old age. (*tsachaq* denotes to laugh Strong's # 6711). The Lord visited Sarah at the set time. She conceived and bore Abraham a son in his old age "at the set time of which God spoke to him" (Genesis 21:1, 2). What would signify the Abrahamic Covenant?

---

[62] L. Grant Luton, *In His Words; Messianic Insights into the Hebrew Alphabet.* (Uniontown, Ohio: Beth Tikkun Publishing 1999) 62,63.

The Rite of Circumcision the Seal of the Abrahamic Covenant

> And God said to Abraham: As for you, you shall keep My covenant, you and your descendants after you throughout their generations. This is my covenant which you shall keep between Me and you and your descendants after you; Every male child among you will be circumcised.   Genesis 17:9,10

The rite of circumcision sealed the Abrahamic Covenant between God, Abraham, and his descendants. Circumcision was a command that God issued to all the male descendants of Abraham, granting them entrance into the Abrahamic Covenant. This sacred ceremony was an outward demonstration of their loyalty and faithfulness to the God of Abraham. It required the cutting away of the flesh of the foreskin, involving the shedding of blood. It was performed on the eighth day (Genesis 21:4). Any man, who failed to obey the commandment of circumcision, would be guilty of breaking the covenant relationship with God. As a result, he would be cut off from the blessings of God. The rite of circumcision of the Old Testament is fulfilled in water baptism in which His people identify with the death, burial, and resurrection of Jesus Christ. [63]

> In Him (Christ) you were also circumcised with a circumcision made without hands, by the putting off the body of the sins of the flesh, by the circumcision of Christ, buried with Him in baptism in which

---

[63] Kevin J. Conner and Ken Malmin, *The Covenants: The Key to God's Relationship With Mankind* (Portland, Oregon: City Bible Publishing, 1983), 38

Kathleen Martinez

you were also raised with Him through faith in the
working of God, who raised Him from the dead.

Colossians 2:11-12.

Having a new life and identity with Christ, (His death, burial,
and resurrection), the faithful reject and turn away from their old
lifestyle. They no longer "walk according to the flesh, but according
to the Spirit" (Romans 1:1). However, the faith of the believers is
often tested as in the case of Abraham.

The Sacrifice of Isaac

> Now it came to pass after these things that God
> tested Abraham and said to him,
>   "Abraham!" And He said, "Here I am." Then
> He said, "take now your son, your only son, Isaac,
> whom you love, and go to the land of Moriah, and
> offer him there as a burnt offering on one of the
> mountains of which I shall tell you."
>
> Genesis 22:1, 2

After having been given Isaac, his only beloved son who was
conceived by his wife Sarah at the advanced age of one hundred
years, God called him by name "Abraham!" Now Abraham
recognizing the Voice of God, promptly responded, "Here I am."
Then God commanded him to take his only beloved son travel up to
the land of Moriah to offer him as a burnt offering on a mountain.
A natural response to God's outlandish directive could have been
shock and disbelief. Obviously, God's request would make no sense
for it seems to contradict His promise of a son through whom He
would establish an everlasting covenant (Genesis 17:19). Now as
Abraham arose early the following morning in obedience to the
Lord his God, he mused that God is trustworthy. If he sacrificed
Isaac, God would have to raise him from the dead (Hebrews 11:18).
So, he held firmly unto his faith during a time of extreme testing.
To his servants, Abraham declared that he and his son were going
up the mountain *to worship* the Lord. As they are ascending to the
place of sacrifice, Isaac asked his father "where is the lamb for a burnt
offering?" His answer came as a direct revelation from God. "My
son, God will provide for Himself the Lamb for a burnt offering."
Now he had recalled that in the Garden of Eden, the Lord God
promised to send a Redeemer. (Genesis 3:15) Moreover, on the night

Kathleen Martinez

that God had initiated a blood covenant with Abraham, He passed between the pieces of the slain animals. In doing so, He obligated Himself to shed His own Blood and thus create an unbroken bond with Abraham and his descendants (Genesis 15:17). Therefore, The Lord God would never break His promise to Abraham and his seed nor would His original plan of redemption be annulled. Therefore, Abraham was able to stand upon the Lord's covenantal promise. He would provide for Himself a Lamb! Who would be the Lamb of God? In John 3:16, Jesus, Himself as the Lamb of God declared, "For God so loved the world that He gave His only begotten Son that whoever believes in Him should not perish, but have everlasting life."

As Abraham bound his son Isaac, laid him on the altar as a burnt offering, and stretched out his hand to slay his beloved son, the Angel of the Lord called out to him from heaven, "Do not lay your hand on the Lad or do anything to him; for I know that you fear God since you have not withheld your son, your only son from Me" (Genesis 22: 12). Then Abraham saw a ram caught in a thicket and offered it up for a burnt offering. Although, the Angel of the Lord suspended the sacrifice of Isaac, God would not spare His Son. According to the Abrahamic Covenant, He would shed His own Blood to save the world. In response, Abraham called the name of the place "The- Lord- Will- Provide" (Genesis 22:14). (YHWH Yireh from the verb *ra'ah* Strong's #7200 to behold, gaze, take heed, look on another, provide). As the Lord Himself saw that Abraham feared Him to the extent that he was willing to sacrifice his only son, He blessed him:

> By Myself I have sworn, says the Lord, because you have done this thing, and have not withheld your son, blessing I will bless you and multiplying I will multiply your descendants as the stars of heaven and as the sand which is on the seashore; and your descendants shall possess the gate of your enemies.

In your seed all the nations of the earth shall be
blessed because you have obeyed My Voice.

Genesis 22:16-18

The legacy of Abraham's faith and obedience would be passed
down to his son Isaac (Genesis 26:1-5), Jacob (Genesis 28:13-15),
and the children of Israel (Exodus 34:10-28) The descendants of
Abraham were called to become a kingdom of priests and a holy
nation (Exodus 19:5, 6). Ultimately, all the families of the earth
would be blessed due to the obedience of this one man who remained
faithful in the time of extreme testing.(Genesis 12:3) Furthermore,
the Abrahamic Covenant would be the sure foundation upon which
all future covenants would be laid.

Throughout history men or women of faith would be tested in
various fiery trials. They have proven to be more than conquerors,
sustained by the power and the presence of God. Through God
Almighty, they are able to overcome all adverse circumstances,
assured of His faithfulness to keep the Abrahamic Covenant. After
four hundred years of slavery in Egypt under the oppressive rule of
Pharaoh, the children of Israel cried out to the God of Abraham,
Isaac, and Jacob for deliverance. Again, the Lord would hear their
cry and send them a deliverer who was called Moses.

Kathleen Martinez

Moses Prophet of God
Whom the Lord Knew Face to Face (Deut.33:10)

> By faith Moses, when he was born, was hidden three months by his parents, because they saw he was a beautiful child, and they were not afraid of the king's command.   Hebrews 11:23.

The book of Exodus opens up with the names of the eleven sons of Israel who came down to Egypt to live in Egypt during a famine of seven years. The Lord God had preserved the household of Israel through Joseph. Joseph, favored by his father Jacob, was sold by his envious brothers to the Ishmaelites for twenty shekels of silver. (Genesis 37:28). In Egypt, Joseph was sold again to Potiphar, an officer of Pharaoh. Potiphar saw that "the Lord was with Joseph and he was a successful man" (Genesis 39:1, 2). Therefore, Potiphar appointed Joseph as overseer of his house. When Joseph was wrongly accused by the wife of Potiphar, he was thrown into prison. However, the Lord was with him and continued to show him favor. Through the Spirit of God, Joseph possessed the extraordinary ability to interpret the dreams of a baker and a cupbearer both serving prison terms. After Joseph interpreted their dreams, they came to pass. They were set free. However, they forgot about Joseph. After two years, Pharaoh had two startling dreams as a warning that there would be a severe famine lasting seven years. The cupbearer remembered a prisoner who had interpreted his dream. Immediately, Pharaoh sent for Joseph who declared that "God will give Pharaoh an answer of peace" (Genesis 41:16). Through his dreams, God had shown Pharaoh that seven years of plenty would be followed by seven years of famine. After revealing the interpretation of his dreams,

Joseph advised Pharaoh to store grain reserved for the seven years of famine. Recognizing the Spirit of wisdom and discernment in Joseph, Pharaoh set him over all the land of Egypt as the prime minister who was second only to his throne. God elevated Joseph to be a preserver of people from many nations including his own family who inhabited land of Canaan. To the family of Joseph, Pharaoh gave the land of Goshen as their dwelling place (Genesis 47:6).

After the death of Joseph and his generation, the children of Israel were very fruitful. The children of Israel increased abundantly, multiplied quickly, and grew mightily in the land of Egypt. Then a new king arose to rule over Egypt. He did not know Joseph (Exodus 1:7, 8). Seeing that the numbers of Israelites far exceeded the Egyptians, the king decided to deal shrewdly with them lest they joined his enemies in war against him. He treated them harshly placing them into hard bondage. As the Egyptians increased their afflictions, the children of Israel greatly multiplied more and more. Now, the king ordered the midwives of Hebrew women to kill the male children. But they feared God and delivered them at the time of their birth.

In his desperation, the new king commanded all God's people to cast every son into the river (Exodus1:22). However, Jochebed, a devoted Jewish mother beholding the beauty of her newborn son, chose to disobey the decree of the king and hid him away for three months. When she could no longer hide her son, she put him in an ark of bulrushes and laid it in the reeds by the riverbank (Exodus 2:1-3). Through her brave action, she was able to preserve her son who would become the deliverer of the nation of Israel.[64] Moreover, his sister Miriam stood by observing the daughter of Pharaoh. While she was bathing at the river, she discovered a Hebrew baby crying and had compassion on him. Immediately, Miriam offered to call one of the Hebrew women to nurse the child. The daughter of

---

[64] Jack W. Hayford, *New Spirit-Filled Life Bible: Kingdom Equipping Through the Power of the Word.* (Nashville, Tennessee: Thomas Nelson, Inc., 2002), 78.

Kathleen Martinez

Pharaoh agreed to allow Miriam to take the child away for a season to be nursed by his mother paying her wages. When the child grew, his mother brought him to Pharaoh's daughter who called his name Moses(*Mosheh* Strong's # 4872 A name derived from the verb *Mashah* # 4871 denoting pull out or draw out of the water rescued to be the lawgiver of Israel). His name depicted his calling to be a rescuer of God's people from Egyptian bondage serving under an oppressive king.

> By faith, Moses, when he became of age, refused to be called the son of Pharaoh's daughter, choosing rather to suffer affliction with the people of God than to enjoy the passing pleasures of sin, esteeming the reproach of Christ greater riches than the treasures in Egypt for he looked to the reward.
>
> Hebrews 11:24-26

> Now it came to pass in those days, when Moses was grown, that he went out to his brethren and looked at their burdens. He saw an Egyptian beating a Hebrew, one of his brethren. So he looked this way and that way and when he saw no one, he killed the Egyptian and hid him in the sand. Exodus 2:11

In his heart, Moses felt a strong identity with his people and chose to suffer with them rather than enjoy a life of sin, wealth, and power as the son of Pharaoh's daughter. Seeing the abuse of one of his brothers by an Egyptian taskmaster, Moses sprang into action and slew him. However, when two Hebrew men were fighting the following day, he confronted one of them, "Why are you striking your companion?" One of the Hebrews replied, "Who made you a prince and a judge over us? Do you intend to kill me as you killed the Egyptian?" Now Moses came to the realization that his own people had witnessed his killing of the Egyptian and rejected his leadership. "Surely this thing is known!" (Exodus 2:14)

Knowing that Pharaoh was seeking to kill him, Moses fled from Egypt and dwelt in the land of Midian. On Mount Horeb, the mountain of God, a miraculous spectacle caught his attention. While he was tending the flock of Jethro, his father-in-law, the Angel of the Lord "appeared to him in a flame of fire from the midst of a bush" (Exodus 3:1, 2). However, the burning bush was not being consumed. Moreover, the Voice of the Lord called out to him from the burning bush and said "Moses, Moses!" The ground upon which Moses stood was holy ground. He was standing in the presence of the Holy One who is God.

Out of reverence, Moses was asked to remove his sandals. Then the Lord identified Himself saying, "I am the God of your father— the God of Abraham, the God of Isaac, and the God of Jacob." In fear, Moses hid his face. With compassion, the Lord announced that He had seen the oppression of His people, heard their cry and knew their sorrow. He came down to deliver them out of Egypt and bring them up to Canaan, the land of promise that He had made to Abraham and his descendants. Therefore, the Lord announced that He was sending him to Pharaoh to bring the children of Israel out of Egypt and to serve Him on this mountain. Furthermore, the Lord promised to be with him. Then in response to his calling, Moses inquired about His Name. Who was sending him? What is His Name? The Lord revealed His eternal Name "I AM THAT I AM" *a'hyah asher a'hyah* that denotes "I shall forever be as I am". This is His Name forever and will be a memorial to all generations (Exodus 3:15) [65] In John 8:58, Yeshua invoked the Name YHVH, "Before Abraham, was, I AM". The Son of God forever identifies Himself with His Father. Traditionally, the Name of the Lord is so sacred that the Jews do not utter it. Instead, they call Him *"Adonai"* Lord!

---

[65] L. Grant Luton, *In His Words; Messianic Insights into the Hebrew Alphabet.* (Uniontown, Ohio: Beth Tikkun Publishing 1999) 6, 7.

Kathleen Martinez

Moses was commanded by the Lord to gather the elders of Israel and declare that 'I AM" has sent me to you.' But Moses was afraid that they would not listen nor believe him. The Lord asked him "What is in your hand?" "A rod." The rod of Moses as the Lord's Rod would perform great and mighty miracles before Pharaoh revealing Himself as the Lord of all the earth. Although God gave him His Rod, Moses held onto his doubts about his calling, making excuses that he was "slow in speech and of tongue" (Exodus 4:10). When Moses asked God to send someone else to speak on his behalf, the anger of the Lord kindled upon him. He would send his brother Aaron to be his spokesman.

> So he shall be your spokesman to the people. And
> he himself shall be as a mouth for you, and you
> shall be to him as God. And you shall take this rod
> in your hand, with which you shall do the signs
> Exodus 4:15-17.

Aaron would be the communicator of God's word to the children of Israel. The Lord assured them that He would be with both of them and would teach them what to do. Now the people, who had long lived under the oppression of Pharaoh as his slaves, would hear that God heard their cry for deliverance and had not forgotten them. He would show Himself mighty through great signs and miracles. Whenever the Lord calls His people to perform signs and miracles, He equips them with the Rod of His power and authority. In response, they offer up their hands in worship and service. They present themselves as willing servants, through whom His work will be accomplished. His strength and power is manifested, as they totally submit to His authority. (*yad* Strong's 3027 denotes hand ; *yadah* Strong's 3034 denotes throw, cast giving thanks). With the Rod of God in his hand, Moses returned to Egypt to go before Pharaoh to give him a firm ultimatum:

Israel is My son, My firstborn… let My son go that
he may serve Me. But if you refuse to let him go,
indeed, I will kill your son, your firstborn
Exodus 4:22, 23.

When Moses and Aaron would came before Pharaoh requesting
to let his people go out into the wilderness to worship the Lord, he
would repeatedly refused to let them go. Pharaoh regarded himself to
be the god ruling over Egypt and all his people. Therefore, he would
not acknowledge the Lord God of Israel.

Thus says the Lord God of Israel: Let my people go,
that they may hold a feast to Me in the wilderness.
And Pharaoh said, "Who is the Lord that I should
obey His Voice to let Israel go? I do not know the Lord
nor will I let Israel go"   Exodus 5:1, 2

In response to Moses and Aaron's request to let the Israelites go
into the wilderness to hold their feast unto the Lord, Pharaoh refused
to obey the Voice of the Lord because he did not know nor did he
recognize the God of the children of Israel. As Pharaoh, he claimed
his right to rule over them having his divine right of kings. Pharaoh
believed that the Egyptian deities had given him absolute power and
authority over all his people. He would not permit his slaves any idle
time to go and worship the Lord their God. As severe punishment,
he greatly increased their toil, laboring longer hours under their
taskmasters who required them to gather their own straw to fulfill
their daily quota making bricks.

Observing the hardness of Pharaoh's heart, hearing the cry
of His people, the Lord assured Moses that He is the Lord who
had appeared to their fathers Abraham, Isaac, and Jacob. As God
Almighty, He had established an everlasting covenant with them
promising to give them and their descendants the land of Canaan
as an inheritance.

Kathleen Martinez

I am the Lord (*YHWH*). I appeared to Abraham, to Isaac, and to Jacob as God Almighty (Genesis 17:1) … I also established My covenant with them to give them the Land of Canaan. (Genesis 15:18) And I have also heard the groaning of the children of Israel whom the Egyptians keep in bondage and I have remembered My covenant. Therefore say to the children of Israel: I am the Lord; I will bring you out from under the burdens of the Egyptians, I will rescue you from their bondage, and I will redeem you with an outstretched arm and with great judgments I will take you as My people and I will be your God. Then you shall know that I am the Lord your God who brings you out from under the burdens of the Egyptians And I will bring you into the land which I swore to give to Abraham, Isaac, and Jacob and I will give it to you as a heritage: I am the Lord   Exodus 6:2-8.

In remembrance of His covenant with their forefathers, He informed His people that He would deliver them from their grueling slavery under Pharaoh. Moreover, He would redeem them with His outstretched arm and with great judgments, performing signs, miracles, and wonders. Moreover, His judgments would come against Pharaoh and his false gods. [66] The Lord God would send out ten plagues smiting the Egyptians, revealing His Sovereign rule over all the nations of the earth. Today, the Lord uses natural disasters to warn His people to shake off their lethargy and apathy. Now is the day of salvation and deliverance for America and the nations of the world. They are to return to Him and repent before judgment

---

[66] Jack W. Hayford, *New Spirit-Filled Life Bible: Kingdom Equipping Through the Power of the Word.* (Nashville, Tennessee: Thomas Nelson, Inc., 2002), 86.

falls upon them and it is too late! Through His devoted ministry and army of deliverers, He desires to perform great miracles to reveal Himself as the Lord of the whole earth! Observe the mighty signs, miracles and wonders the Lord did through Moses.

The Revelation of the Lord God Through Ten Plagues

Waters turned to Blood. God sent out His first plague when Moses lifted up his rod, and struck the waters. They turned to blood. However, Pharaoh was not moved by this first plague. Exodus (7:20)

Frogs The second plague came about as Aaron stretched out his hand over the waters of Egypt. Frogs were linked with the goddess Heqt.[67] They entered into the houses of the Egyptians and Pharaoh's palace. (Exodus 8:6) Then Pharaoh called Moses to entreat the Lord to take them away. The Lord God of Israel answered the prayer of Moses and the frogs died leaving a stench in the land. However, Pharaoh refused to humble himself and acknowledge that Yahweh was Lord over Egypt.

Lice The third plague followed as Aaron stretched out his hand striking the dust of the earth causing lice to come forth afflicting both men and beasts throughout the land of Egypt. (Exodus 8: 16) But Pharaoh continued to hardened his heart, while his magicians acknowledged that this plague was "the Finger of God" (Exodus 8:19).

Flies Again, Moses and Aaron appealed to Pharaoh to let his people go, or face the fourth plague. A thick swarm of flies would descend upon the people and enter into their houses. Their lands were corrupted by the flies. However, due to the protection of the Lord over His people in the land of Goshen, there were no flies. In response, Pharaoh called upon Moses to intercede for him, promising to let the people go into the wilderness to sacrifice to the Lord their God. (Exodus 8: 28), But when the flies were removed, again Pharaoh refused to let them go.

Livestock Diseased When Pharaoh did not release His people

---

[67] Ibid.

to serve Him, He brought the fifth plague upon the livestock of Egyptians causing a devastation of their economy. However, no disease came upon the livestock's of the Israelites. (Exodus 9:6) When he saw the death of his livestock, Pharaoh's heart became hardened and obstinate.

Boils The sixth plague came forth from the ashes that Moses and Aaron scattered toward the heavens before the presence of Pharaoh, afflicting man and beast with painful boils breaking out as sores. However, Pharaoh refused to heed the Voice of the Lord. (Exodus 9:10)

Hail Seventh plague that had never been seen previously in Egypt rained down heavily upon it. Pharaoh exalted himself against the Lord's people refusing to let them go. Through this severe plague, the Lord was letting Pharaoh know that there was no God like Him. Moreover, He is in complete control of nature over all the earth (Exodus 9:20).

Locusts Then the eighth plague sent by God to be another amazing sign to the Egyptians that they "may know that I am the Lord." Causing further catastrophic effects on their agriculture, a dark cloud of locusts consumed every tree of the field. Moreover, these menacing creatures filled all of their houses. While his people endured incredible devastation, Pharaoh continued to be stubborn, standing his ground, refusing to let God's people go. He would not humble himself before the Lord (Exodus10:13).

Darkness The ninth plague came upon the Egyptians as a heavy darkness that could be felt, covering the land of Egypt for three days. During this time, the children of Israel had light in their dwellings. Reluctantly, Pharaoh agreed to permit the Israelites to go serve the Lord, but without their flocks, their herds and their children. When Moses insisted that the livestock would go with them, Pharaoh sternly warned him to leave his presence or face death (Exodus10:22, 24, and 29). Moses did not fear Pharaoh for His Invisible God was revealing Himself as the Light to His people so that they are able to overcome the darkness in the world (John 1:5).

Kathleen Martinez

Death of the Firstborn The Lord announced to Moses that He would send one more plague over Egypt, the death of the firstborn. Thus, the Lord would demonstrate that He is the Giver of Life who is greater than Osiris, the Egyptian god.[68] Upon the death of their firstborn, Pharaoh called for Moses and Aaron to arise, and go out into the wilderness to serve the Lord. Upon the urgent request of the people of Israel, the Egyptians gave them silver and gold jewelry and clothing. The plundering of their Egyptian oppressors was a just payment for their bitter enslavement of 430 years. (Exodus 12: 31, 32, 40). The Lord had promised Abraham that his descendants would be sent out of Egypt with great possessions (Genesis 15:14). This momentous night of deliverance when the Lord brought His people out of Egypt would be celebrated forever with the institution of the Feast of Passover. This Feast of Passover would mark the commencement of the sacred Jewish calendar, commemorating the Lord's protection and preservation of His firstborn the children of Israel.

---

[68] Jack W. Hayford, *New Spirit-Filled Life Bible: Kingdom Equipping Through the Power of the Word*. (Nashville, Tennessee: Thomas Nelson, Inc., 2002), 90.

The Institution of the Passover

> Now the Lord spoke to Moses and Aaron in the land of Egypt saying, "This month shall be your beginning of months; it shall be the first month of the year to you. Speak to all the congregation of Israel, saying on the tenth of this month, every man shall take for himself a lamb according to the house of his father, a lamb for a household… Now you shall keep it until the fourteenth day of the same month. Then the whole assembly of the congregation of Israel shall kill it at twilight. And shall take some of the blood and put it on the doorposts and on the lintel of the houses where they shall eat it Exodus 12:1-7

During the Passover on the tenth day of the month, a lamb was taken by every man for his household to be offered up as a blood sacrifice. On the fourteenth day of the same month at twilight, the whole assembly of the congregation of Israel would kill the lamb and apply some of its blood to the doorposts of their houses. The lamb that is without blemish depicts and foreshadows Christ as the Passover Lamb of God. On the day of the Feast of Passover, the Father offered the Blood of His beloved Son. He was faithful to keep His promise to Abraham. During the ritual of the Abrahamic Covenant, the Lord had passed between the rows of slain animals, vowing to offer Himself as the one and only sacrifice who would shed His own Blood to deliver humanity from death. (Genesis 15:17).

On the night of Passover, the congregation of Israel took the blood of the lamb and applied it to the doorposts of their houses. When the Lord passed over the land of Egypt, He killed the firstborn. Moreover, He was executing judgment against the gods of Egypt.

When He saw the blood as a visible sign upon the doorposts of the houses of His people, He passed over delivering them from the plague of death.

The historical event of the Passover foreshadows the supernatural deliverance of His people who put their trust in Christ for salvation. When they pray in a spirit of humility requesting God for forgiveness, they are cleansed by the Blood of Jesus. As they surrender their lives to Jesus as their Lord and Savior, they are passing from death into eternal life. By faith, they are applying His Blood to the doorposts of their hearts, trusting fully in His work at Calvary. For their deliverance, they look to Jesus, the Son of God. He was appointed by His Father as the One "who should die for the people and not that the whole nation should perish" (John 11:50). After the children of Israel were thrust out of Egypt into the wilderness, another supernatural event at the Red Sea occurred

The Triumph of the Lord over Pharaoh at the Red Sea

As the Lord led them into the wilderness of the Red Sea, He manifested His glorious presence in a pillar of cloud by day and a pillar of fire by night (Exodus 13:18, 21). Again, the Lord hardened the heart of Pharaoh who arose to pursue them with his army riding furiously on horses and chariots. When the children of Israel beheld Pharaoh and his army rapidly advancing to overtake them, they responded in fear. Moses commanded them, "Do not be afraid. Stand still and see the salvation of the Lord" (Exodus 14; 13). Then he stretched out his hand with his rod ever the Red Sea to deliver the Israelites. During the night time, the Lord turned the sea into dry land, employing a strong east wind in demonstration of His power over the natural elements of the earth. As the waters stood up like a wall, His people quickly crossed over the sea on dry land. In an attempt to pursue and overtake them, the Egyptian army drove their chariots into the sea. The Lord, who is a Mighty Man of war, removed their chariot wheels, and caused the depths of the sea to overflow them so that they sank down like lead and drowned in the Red Sea. Then Moses and the children of Israel danced and sang a joyous song of triumph to the Lord celebrating His victory. He triumphed gloriously over the enemy and saved His people. Today, He is able to defeat all enemies who rise up against His people!

The Formation of a New Nation
of Priests at Mount Sinai

> And Moses went up to God and the Lord called him from the mountain saying, "Thus shall you say to the house of Jacob, and tell the children of Israel. 'You have seen what I did to the Egyptians and how I bore you on eagles' wings and brought you to Myself. Now therefore, if you will indeed obey My voice and keep My covenant, then you shall be a special treasure to Me above all people, for all the earth is Mine. And you shall be to Me a kingdom of priests and a holy nation.   Exodus 19:3-6.

After living in the Sinai wilderness for forty years, Moses was prepared to lead the children of Israel into the promise land. During this lengthy time, Moses cultivated an intimate personal relationship with YWVH. Since the day that Moses met with Him at the burning bush, he would commune with the Lord face to face. He called Moses to meet with Him on the mountain of Sinai. The Lord God told Moses to speak to His people that He bore them and carried them on eagle's wings of the Angel of His Presence (Isaiah 63:9). As the Almighty God, He demonstrated His power to deliver His people from their enemies, He bore them carrying them on the wings of His Presence (*Kanaph* Strong's # 3671 denoting an overspreading wing of a bird or an extremity of a garment). Moreover, His wings overshadowed them as a place of refuge and a fortress.

Why did He choose the children of Israel? He chose the children of Israel for Himself to be unto Him a special treasure above all the nations. (*segullah* Strong's # 5459 denotes possession, personal property, special treasure.) Just as a man boasts about his wealth and possessions, God records in a book of remembrance those who fear and obey Him. He refers to them as His "jewels" in Malachi 3:17. At Mount Sinai, He chose them to be His kingdom of priests and a holy nation (Exodus 19:6).

However, He would be their God only if they would obey His voice and keep His covenant. Through a thick cloud, the Lord would descend to the top of the mountain where He would speak with Moses. Standing at the base of the mountain, the people would hear His Voice speaking to him so that they would believe that Moses was a chosen prophet who was sent by God. Moses instructed His people to spend two days consecrating themselves, washing their garments and abstaining from sexual relations. The children of Israel were to fully dedicate themselves to become a holy nation of God.

On the third day, God descended upon His holy mountain to speak with Moses face to face. When the Lord descended upon Mount Sinai, it was covered in smoke and fire. He solemnly warned him to not allow the people to ascend the mountain less they perish. Therefore, Moses set boundaries so that the children of Israel would not perish in the presence of God. At the long blast of the trumpet, they trembled in fear before His presence. Moses descended from the mountain to the people as the Lord spoke Ten Words, the Ten Commandments as His timeless principles governing their relationships with Him as their God and with one another. [69]

---

[69] Jack W. Hayford, *New Spirit-Filled Life Bible: Kingdom Equipping Through the Power of the Word.* (Nashville, Tennessee: Thomas Nelson, Inc., 2002) 102.

The Ten Commandments the Universal Law of God (Exodus 20)

Before the children of Israel, God spoke the Ten Commandments, the Ten Words as their national deity before entering into covenant with them.[70] Whenever God speaks a word, His Word is a command and not a mere suggestion. The purpose of man is to fear God and keep His commandments. Through obedience to His commandments, one honors and reveres Him (Ecclesiastes 12:13). The Ten Commandments are eternal moral laws that guide all of humanity in a proper relationship with God and with one another.

The first four commandments are laws concerning men's relationship with God who clearly states His identity and sovereignty over His creation and His people. In the first commandment, He revealed Himself as the deity who delivered them from Egyptian bondage:

> I am the Lord your God who brought you out of the land of Egypt out of the house of bondage. You shall have no other gods before Me.   Exodus 20:1, 2

In the writings of the prophets, He declared that He is the Lord God who made the earth and created man. The Lord said to Cyrus, a pagan ruler, that there is no god beside Him.

> Thus says the Lord to His anointed, To Cyrus, "I am the Lord and there is no other. There is no God besides Me." The Lord declares that He is the

---

[70] Pat Robertson, *The Ten Offenses: Reclaim the Blessings of the Ten Commandments*.(Nashville, Tennessee: Integrity Publishers,2004) 59.

Creator who made the earth and created man on it.

Isaiah 45: 1, 4, 5, 12.

Through the prophet Isaiah, the Lord spoke to Cyrus, king of Persia, that He would anoint him to be His servant. Through a decree of Cyrus, the Jews shall be allowed to return to their land to rebuild their temple in Jerusalem. To this pagan ruler who worshiped other gods, God disclosed Himself as the God of Israel and Creator of the earth and humanity. There is no other god beside Him. (Isaiah 45:5, 12).

During the reign of Jehoiakim, Jeremiah received a word from the Lord of hosts, the God of Israel who declared that He is the Creator of the earth and its inhabitants:

I have made the earth, the man and the beast...
by My great power and by My outstretched arm.

Jeremiah 27:5,

The Lord God of Hosts and God of Israel is worthy of praise and highest honor as Creator and Redeemer. There is no god who surpasses Him in greatness, power and authority! Happy is he who has the God of Jacob for his help, whose hope is in the Lord God who made heaven and earth, the sea and all that is in them (Psalm 146:5, 6). But woe (judgment) unto those who bow down and serve other gods.

You shall not make for yourself a carved image— any likeness of anything that is in heaven above, or that is in the earth beneath, or that is in the water under the earth. You shall not bow down nor serve them. For I, the Lord your God, am a jealous God visiting the iniquity of the fathers upon the children to the third and fourth generations of those who

Kathleen Martinez

hate Me, but showing mercy to thousands to those
who love me and keep my commandments
Exodus 20:4-6.

The Lord God will not tolerate idolatry or any carved image that bears any likeness of anything in heaven or on earth. Through Isaiah, the Lord proclaims, "I am the Lord, that is My Name and MY glory I will not give to another, nor My praise to carved images" (Isaiah 42:8). Because humanity is made in the image and likeness of God, no man shall worship carved images. The Lord God created humanity to worship Him and Him alone. Whatever a man worships becomes his master, a tyrant who demands more and more of his time, talent, and treasures. Sadly, he becomes more and more conformed to the image and likeness of his idol. Therefore, God is a jealous God (*qanna'* Strong's # 7067 denotes jealousy of God who punishes those who hate him to the third and fourth generations). On the other hand, He desires to show mercy to thousands who love Him and keep His commandments. Moreover, His people honor the Name of the Lord God by living a godly lifestyle.

You shall not take the Name of the Lord in vain, for
the Lord will not hold him guiltless who takes His
Name in vain
Exodus 20:7.

Those who claim to be believers in the Lord, but choose to live a carnal lifestyle, take His Name in vain. In their ungodly conduct, they degrade His divine Name, and character in the eyes of men. Furthermore, the ungodly make light of His Name using it as a swear word in everyday language. Having no fear of God, they abase Him, compromising their faith, turning many nonbelievers away from Him. Therefore, Paul exhorts the Corinthians to separate themselves from the evil ways of this world and not be influenced nor drawn into pagan cultures.

In his letter to the Corinthians, Paul exhorts
them saying, "Come out from among them and
be separate, says the Lord. Do not touch what is
unclean. And I will receive you. I will be a Father
to you. And you shall be My sons and daughters,
says the Lord Almighty   II Corinthians 6:17, 18.

Those who sanctify themselves are dedicating their lives to exalt
the Name of the Lord. As His witnesses, they are to walk worthy
of God, answering His call to enter into His kingdom and glory.
(I Thessalonians 2:12) Living in the midst of a perverse generation,
His people are pure, godly, and just in all their ways. As a result,
their Father receives and accepts them into His Kingdom as His
sons and daughters.

Moreover, they obey the law of the Sabbath keeping it holy by
setting aside one day a week to observe the Sabbath of the Lord. The
seventh day is a sign that He is the Lord who sanctifies His people.
(Exodus 31:12- 18). They dedicate time to be with the Lord to grow in
their covenant relationship with Him and one another. It is vital for their
health and well being of His people to enjoy a day of rest, to know Him
in an intimate personal relationship, to experience joy in His presence,
and to be refreshed in an atmosphere filled with praise and worship.

Remember the Sabbath day to keep it holy. Six
days you shall labor and do all your work. But the
seventh day is the Sabbath of the Lord your God
                                          Exodus 20:8-11.

In the six days of creation, "the Lord God made the heavens and
the earth, the sea and all that is in them" On the seventh day, He
ceased from His work. (yowm Strong's #3117 denotes a day, sunrise
to sunset, an age, time or period [71]) Elohim sanctified the seventh

---

[71] Hugh Ross, *The Genesis Question: Scientific Advances and the Accuracy of Genesis.* (Colorado Springs, Colorado: NavPress, 1998) 196.

day. . He established it holy as a day of rest. How long does this day last? It lasts until the time when Jesus will return for His glorious church. (I Thessalonians 4:13-18)

> There remains therefore a rest for the people of
> God. For he who has entered his rest has himself
> also ceased from his works as God did from His
> Hebrews 4:9,10.

By faith, God's people may enter into His rest today. Now is the day of salvation. Rest implies having full confidence that Christ has completed His work at the Cross for their redemption. Furthermore, Christ has invited His disciples to come to Him to be relieved of their labor under a religious system of legalism with an endless list of rules, and regulations. (Matthew 11:29, 30) Through a personal relationship with Jesus, His disciples are not able to earn their salvation through good works. Instead, they are to put their trust in the complete work that Christ accomplished for them at Calvary. Furthermore, Jesus teaches His followers to be like Him, having a gentle and humble spirit. He desires to do His work in and through them. His believers surrender their will to the Lordship of Christ, and submit to the Holy Spirit who leads them to the full knowledge of His perfect will. When God's people are obedient to His will, His Spirit empowers and equips them to accomplish His plan and purpose to spread the Gospel of the Kingdom of God to all nations. (Matthew 28:19) They are called as a royal priesthood to exercise dominion on earth to bring His heavenly kingdom down to earth!

Through their redemption in Christ and their empowerment of the Holy Spirit, believers no longer yield to the temptations of the flesh nor do they fall under the influenced of the world. In the fear of the Lord, they walk in obedience, observing His commandments all their days. Through their obedience, the Lord God promises to reward them and their children with a long and prosperous life.

(Deuteronomy 6: 1, 2) The Lord commanded parents to instruct their children to love Him with all their heart, soul, and strength so that they would learn to walk His in the ways. Children who honor and obey their parents shall live long on earth. (Exodus 20:12). They will not commit murder, adultery, steal, bear false witness or covet their neighbor's possessions. For love does no harm to their neighbor. (Romans 13:10)

Until Jesus came to redeem humanity from sin and death, the children of Israel lived under the law. In the Old Testament, obeying the law was an external act of compliance to the will of God. Submitting to the Ten Words of the Lord was to be a heartfelt act of worship. The Lord God gave them His commandments because they were lawless, rebellious, and disobedient. Beholding the overwhelming presence of the Lord God at the foot of Mount Sinai, they refused to enter into a personal and intimate relationship with Him. Without a close personal relationship with the Lord, His laws were viewed as external regulations that were impossible to observe. Therefore, the purpose of the Law of Moses was to convince them of their need of a Redeemer who would come to set them. Sadly, the children of Israel quickly turn aside from the Lord in disobedience to His second commandment molding a golden calf as their god.

Turning Aside from the Lord
Molding a Golden Calf

Moses was delayed coming down from Mount Sinai when God gave him the two tablets of the Testimony (Exodus 32:1). The Ten Commandments had been written with the finger of God on tablets of stone. (Exodus 31:18) The people who believed that Moses had died on the mountain, requested Aaron to make a god who would go before them. Aaron molded a golden calf to be the god who brought them out of Egypt. Enraged by the rebellion of His stiff-necked people, the Lord threatened to consume them and create a new nation with Moses. When Moses interceded for His people, reminding the Lord of His covenant that He had made with Abraham, Isaac, and Israel to multiply and give to them the land of Canaan, the Lord relented from destroying them. Thus, through intercession Moses acted as a mediator between God and His people to restore their relationship with Him.

Moses pitched a tabernacle of meeting outside the camp. There, "the Lord spoke to Moses face to face as a man speaks to his friend" (Exodus 32:11). He sought to know His ways that he might find grace for his nation "Your people." The Lord assuring of His favor and grace said, "My Presence will go with you, and I will give you rest" (Verse 14). Moreover, the Lord renewed His Covenant with His people, promising to drive out the inhabitants of the land. Again He restated His admonition not to mold or worship other gods (Exodus 34:10). In obedience to the Lord's command, Moses wrote down the words of the covenant that He had made with him and Israel. (Exodus 34:27).

The Children of Israel
Fear God's Presence

When they heard the Voice of God on Mount Sinai, they trembled and refused to be in His presence, afraid that they would perish. The people requested that Moses would speak to them God's words. Then Moses said that He had revealed His Presence to "test" the people (*nasah* Strong's #5254 to test, try and tempt them to see how they would respond)[72] Throughout their wanderings in the wilderness, the people would tempted God ten times and would not heed His Voice (Numbers 14: 22). At Marah, the Lord tested them to see if they would seek Him. When they were unable to drink the bitter water, their immediate response was to grumble and complain against Moses saying, "What shall we drink?" Because they lacked faith in the Lord as their provider, they refused to call upon Him. Then the Lord established a new statute showing Moses a tree that he would cast into the water to heal it. The tree foreshadows the Cross of Jesus that would bring healing to His people. If they diligently took heed to the Voice of the Lord their God, do what is right in His sight, give ear to His commandments, and keep all His statutes, He would put none of the diseases of the Egyptians on them. As their healer, the Lord declared His Name, "I am the Lord who heals you" (Exodus 15:26). *Yahweh –Ropheka* (*Rophe* Strong's #7495 Hebrew participle denotes One who heals) Those who are in a covenant relationship with the Lord, receive healing when they are diligent to hear His Voice and obey His commandments!

Ascending up to the mountain to commune with God, Moses received the words of the Lord and spoke them to the people. They agreed to obey them. Then he built an altar to offered up burnt

---

[72] Jack W. Hayford, *New Spirit-Filled Life Bible: Kingdom Equipping Through the Power of the Word.* (Nashville, Tennessee: Thomas Nelson, Inc., 2002) 747.

Kathleen Martinez

offerings and sprinkle its blood upon it. He wrote down all the words of the Lord in the Book of the Covenant, and read it before the people who promised to obey them. Afterwards, he sprinkled the blood on the people as the blood of the covenant which the Lord had made with them. (Exodus 24:3-8) Moreover, Moses was given the tablets of stone upon which were written the law and commandments on the mountain. (Exodus 14:12) Moreover, Moses received instructions to build a Tabernacle for His dwelling place.

The Ordinances of Divine Service and the Earthly Sanctuary

In Exodus 25-27, the Lord presented Moses a pattern for a tabernacle to be an earthly sanctuary that would be built so that the Lord may dwell in the midst of His people. "And let them make Me a sanctuary that I may dwell among them according to all that I show you, that is the pattern of the Tabernacle and the pattern of all its furnishings" (Exodus 25:8,9; Exodus 26:30) On the mountain, Moses was received His instructions "when he was about to make the tabernacle... He said, 'See that you make all things according to the pattern shown you on the mountain.' (Hebrews 8:5). The tabernacle was to be in a central location where His people would meet with the Lord to worship Him. ("*Ohel Moed*" the Tent of Meeting (Exodus 27:21). In the Garden of Eden, the Lord would meet with Adam in the cool of the day to commune with him and be involved in every part of his life (Genesis 3:8). The Garden of Eden was a place in which humanity would converse with the Lord face to face. Like in the Garden of Eden, the Tabernacle of Moses was built to be a sanctuary where the children of Israel would approach the Presence of the Lord to offer Him their gifts, voluntary offerings and sacrifices. In the wilderness, the Lord instructed Moses to speak to the children of Israel to bring Him an offering of gold, silver bronze, blue, purple, scarlet thread, ram skins, badger skins oil and spices. The children of Israel willingly brought Him these offerings as an act of worship to supply materials with which to build the tabernacle.

The tabernacle would house the Ark of the Testimony, a wooden chest overlaid in gold, a symbol of God's throne placed in the Holy of Holies. The mercy seat, guarded by two angels (Cherubim) made of pure gold, would be set on the top of the chest. "There I will meet with you and I will speak with you from above the mercy seat from between the two cherubim which are on the Ark of the Testimony" (Exodus 15:22). Within the Tabernacle was the Holy Place that contained a Table of Shewbread symbolizing Christ as the Bread of Life, the Gold Lampstand symbolizing Christ as the Light of the world, and the Altar of Incense symbolizing prayer (Psalm 141:2). [73] Aaron was consecrated as priest "that he may minister to Me as priest; Aaron and Aaron's sons" (Exodus 28:1) "Appointed by the Lord for men in things pertaining to God that he may offer both gifts and sacrifices for sins" (Hebrews 5:1). According to the writer of Hebrews, Aaron had to offer sacrifices repeatedly for the sins of the people and for himself. (Hebrews 10:11) However, in contrast to the Aaronic priesthood, the High Priesthood of Christ is everlasting. He appeared once and for all offering Himself as a sacrifice to take away the sins of His people. "And it is appointed for men to die once, but after the judgment, so Christ was offered once to bear the sins of many" (Hebrews 9:26-28). In their appreciation for His redemptive work, they must guard their hearts in love and obedience.

---

[73] Jack W. Hayford, *New Spirit-Filled Life Bible: Kingdom Equipping Through the Power of the Word.* (Nashville, Tennessee: Thomas Nelson, Inc., 2002) 108-112,.

Do Not Harden Your Hearts In Fear Psalm 95:8-11

Today, if you hear His voice, "Do not harden your hearts as in the rebellion, as in the day of trial in the wilderness, when your fathers tested Me; They tried Me, though the saw my work. For forty years I was grieved with that generation, And said, 'It is a people who go astray in their hearts, and they do not know my ways.' So I swore in My wrath, 'They shall not enter My rest.'"   Psalm 95:8-11

What advantage then has the Jew or what is the profit of circumcision? Much in every way! Chiefly because to them was committed the oracles of God. For what if some did not believe? Will their unbelief make the faithfulness of God without effect? Certainly not! Let God be true but every man a liar.   Romans 3:1-4.

In the wilderness, the children of Israel heard the actual Voice of the Lord at Mount Sinai. Through the leadership of Moses, they entered into covenantal relationship with the Lord who presented His universal moral laws in the Ten Commandments, built a Tabernacle as a meeting place, and appointed the Aaronic priesthood to offer voluntary gifts and sacrifices for their sins. Moreover, His people had observed His signs and wonders and miracles in Egypt and the opening of the Red Sea. When the Lord called them to enter into the land of Canaan to conquer its inhabitants and take possession of their inheritance that had been promised under the Abrahamic Covenant, they hardened their hearts. They turned aside in fear and unbelief upon hearing the negative report of ten spies whom they had sent out to survey the land. These wicked men described the inhabitants as giants great in stature. They discouraged the people with a "bad report" convincing them that they would not be able to go up against them. In spite of the power and presence of the Lord, they declared that His people would be helpless like grasshoppers. Sadly, the congregation chose to believe a negative report. Moreover, they refused to listen to Caleb. He had an excellent spirit and a positive outlook of faith toward the Lord. Therefore, Caleb encouraged them, "Let us go up at once and take possession, for we are well able to overcome it." (Numbers 13:30). Due to their lack of faith in the Lord God, a Great and Almighty Warrior who had brought them a glorious victory over Pharaoh and his army at the Red Sea, they rejected Him. Furthermore, they complained against Moses, stating that they would have been better off dying in Egypt or in the wilderness. They threatened to rebel against the Lord and turn back to Egypt. Again Caleb cried out saying "Do not rebel against the Lord nor fear the people of the Land, for they are bread, their protection has departed from them and THE LORD IS WITH US. DO NOT FEAR THEM." In spite of Caleb's desperate plea to trust in their God, they refused to acknowledge His promise to be with them to defeat their enemies in a glorious victory. As a result, the Lord was sorely grieved over their lack of faith:

> The Lord said, "How long will these people reject Me? And how long will they not believe Me with all the signs which I have performed among them?" (Exodus 14:11) "How long shall I bear with this evil congregation who complain against Me? ... Say to them, "As long as I live," says the Lord, "just as you have spoken in My hearing, so I will do to you. The carcasses of you who have complained against Me shall fall in this wilderness ...Except for Caleb and

Joshua, you shall by no means enter the land which
I swore I would make you dwell in"

Numbers 14:27-30

How long would the Lord tolerate these stiff-necked people who had no loving heart that believed in Him? Instead, they declared their own demise causing His Hand of judgment to fall upon them. Therefore, the Lord sentenced this faithless generation to wander and die in the wilderness for forty long years. Because of their negative attitude toward Him, they never set foot in the promise land to claim their inheritance. However, under the strong and willing leadership of Joshua and Caleb, a new generation arose with faith in the Lord God. After viewing the tragic deaths of the previous generation, they were eager to enter into the land, conquer the inhabitants, and take possession of their inheritance.

Today, His people in America must be willing to embrace the challenge of taking hold of the promises of God, take back America, standing up against their enemies who threaten to take away their heritage of religious freedom. They must be willing to rise up and defend their Christian faith, and take authority over the spirit of hate and violence that divides the nation. The Lord is looking for a people who are willing to exercise their political rights and take their responsibility to vote and elect men and women into high office to defend life, liberty, and the pursuit of happiness. They must fight for the soul of America, destroy their enemies here and abroad, and reclaim their Christian heritage. Let them be courageous like David who brought down Goliath, the giant who taunted the army of the Lord and challenged one man to defeat him in combat. Under the anointing of the Spirit of God, David boldly faced Goliath in the Name of the Lord, killed him, and won a great victory for Israel. Let the army of God rise up, take a stand against their enemies, refute their violent accusations and lies, and defeat them through prayer, fasting and action led by the mighty power of the Spirit of God. Let His people who are called by His Name, humble themselves in

Kathleen Martinez

prayer, seek the Lord, repent of their apathy and self-centeredness, and openly contend for their freedom in every phase of American life.

> No weapon formed against you shall prosper and every tongue that rises against you in judgment, you shall condemn. This is the heritage of the servants of the Lord and their righteousness is from Me says the Lord   Isaiah 54:17.

Will the Lord eventually find a people who have a heart after Him? He is seeking people who will put their trust in Him, hear His Voice, and obey His commandments. There was a man who loved the Lord with his whole heart. He was a genuine worshipper who exalted and praised the Name of the Lord his God. His psalms were dedicated to the glory of the Lord his God. Moreover, he was a mighty warrior who went out and conquered all the enemies of Israel. The Lord appointed this young shepherd and anointed him to be a just ruler over His people Israel!

David a Man after God's Own Heart His Grace and Mercy

> Now the Lord said to Samuel, "How long will you mourn for Saul, seeing I have rejected him from reigning over Israel? Fill your horn with oil, and go; I am sending you to Jesse, the bethlehemite. For I have provided Myself a king among his sons.
>
> I Samuel 16:1.

In I Samuel 8, the Israelites demanded a king who would lead them into battle to defeat their enemies. The prophet Samuel reluctantly granted their request. In actuality, the people were rejecting the Lord as their King who had reigned over them since the day He brought them out of Egypt. (I Samuel 8:7). However, Samuel sternly warned the people that the man, whom they elected to be their king, would be an oppressive ruler who would draft them into his army as officers. He would confiscate their possessions, "take their best fields, vineyards, and olive groves, and give them to his servants... take your male servants and female servants" (I Samuel 8:5, 11)

Upon seeking the Lord in prayer, Samuel was sent to anoint Saul, a brilliant commander from the tribe of Benjamin (I Samuel 9:16). In the natural realm, this man appeared to be a very desirable leader in the eyes of men. "From his shoulders upward, he was taller than any of the people" (I Samuel 9:1, 2). After he was anointed by Samuel as the king of Israel, God "gave him another heart...the Spirit of God came upon him and he prophesied" (I Samuel 10:9, 10). As the first king over Israel, he enjoyed the praises of his people for his victories over Moab, Ammon, Edom, Philistines, and the Amalekites (I Samuel 14:47, 48).

However, Saul had a deeply flawed character that would lead to his downfall. Saul had been given instructions by Samuel to wait seven days until he came to him at Gilgal to offer burnt offerings and make sacrifices of peace offerings (I Samuel 10: 8). Unfortunately, Saul did not follow Samuel's instructions to wait for him for seven days. As the Philistines were gathering at Mishmash to fight the Israelites, his army fled in fear from Gilgal. In distress, Saul was compelled in his spirit to offer the burnt offerings in supplication unto the Lord. Only a few moments later, Samuel appeared and rebuked King Saul for disobeying the commandment of the Lord. His kingdom would be taken away from him and given to another man after His own heart. Rejecting the word of the Lord was an act of rebellion that put an end to Saul's kingdom. A better man would be chosen by the Lord to rule over Israel for he would obey His commandments.

> For the Lord has sought for Himself a man after His own heart and the Lord has commanded him to be commander over his people because you have not kept what the Lord commanded you
> I Samuel 13:14.

> For rebellion is as the sin of witchcraft. And stubbornness is as iniquity and idolatry. Because you have rejected the word of the Lord, He has rejected you from being king   I Samuel 15:23.

> How long will you mourn for Saul, seeing that I have rejected him from reigning over Israel? Fill your horn with oil and go: I am sending you to Jesse the Bethlehemite. For I have provided Myself a king among his sons   I Samuel 16:1.

As a weak leader King Saul caved under the pressure seeing his men fleeing away from him in fear. While facing an upcoming battle with the Philistines, Saul called for a burnt offering and peace offerings. In a sudden state of unreasonable terror, he failed to wait Samuel. Only Samuel was authorized as a priest unto God to offer burnt sacrifices. When King Saul transgressed beyond his boundary of authority, he disobeyed the command of the Lord, His Supreme Commander. In so doing, he failed to submit to the authority of God. Therefore, his kingdom would be given to a better man, a man after God's own heart. The Lord instructed Samuel to anoint the king who would be His choice to rule and reign over His people. Moreover, his kingdom would be without end endure forever.

The Anointing of David In the Midst of His Brothers

In I Samuel 16, the Lord sent Samuel to Jesse the Bethlehemite from the tribe of Judah. Who was Jesse? In Ruth 4, the genealogy of David is recorded. Jesse is listed as the grandson of Ruth and Boaz (Ruth 4:18-21). In the story of Ruth, a young widow from Moab left her homeland with Naomi, her mother-in-law, to be joined and united with her people in Bethlehem, Judah. By faith, Ruth put her trust in the Lord God of Israel. She found favor and refuge under the shadow of His wings as the Lord God supplied her provision and protection in the field of Boaz. Boaz was a close relative of her late husband (Ruth 2:12, 13; Ruth 3:2).

Naomi instructed Ruth to seek Boaz as her redeemer kinsman. At midnight, she was to lie at his feet and request that he spread the corner of his garment over her, "Take your maidservant under your wing for you are a close relative" (Ruth 3:9). (*Goel* one who redeems, acting as a redeemer kinsman, a participle from the verb *Ga'al* Strong's # 1350 to redeem to be the next of kin who marries his widow). Under the Levirate Law in Deuteronomy 25:5-10, the redeemer kinsman was the nearest relative. He was required to marry the widow of his deceased brother who was childless in order to preserve his seed.[74] The story of Ruth is a beautiful illustration of God's gracious deliverance and acceptance of all who come to Jesus Christ, the Redeemer Kinsman. By faith, foreigners may enter into His family and become members of His household. God the Father receive them as His beloved children (Ephesians 2:19). As one who was lost and helpless, Ruth received redemption through a wealthy relative. He was empowered to purchase her from poverty

---

[74] Merrill F. Unger, *Unger's Bible Dictionary*. (Chicago, Illinois: The Moody Press, 1971), 700.

and widowhood. Furthermore, Ruth exemplified the redeemed as His special people who are chosen to enter into a close, intimate personal relationship with their Redeemer-Kinsman. As the bride of Christ, they are joined unto Him and shall rule and reign with Him in His kingdom forever.

> To Him who loved us and washed us from our sins in His own blood, and has made us kings and priests to His God and Father to Him be glory and dominion forever and ever   Revelation 1:5,6.

Through Jesus Christ, their Redeemer who loved them and washed them from their sins in His own Blood, they are conformed to His divine image and likeness to be His royal priesthood. They are a beautiful reflection of His divine nature. In their worship and adoration of Him, they attribute to God the Father glory and dominion both now and throughout eternity! Just as Boaz, a wealthy Kinsman, was able and willing to purchase Ruth to be his wife, Jesus Christ was willing to lay down His own life for His bride. He shed His Blood at the cross to create for Himself a glorious church without spot or wrinkle. Today, He has made His special people to be His kings and priests who love Him. They are devoted worshippers offering their praises to His God and Father.

In the early period of the patriarchs, the Lord's vision of a royal priesthood was revealed to Abraham through his encounter with Melchizadek, King of Righteousness and Priest of God the Most High (Genesis 14). Through the Abrahamic Covenant, the Lord God had blessed Abraham to be exceedingly fruitful, and from him, God would bring forth nations and kings. (Genesis 17:6; Genesis 35:11). Throughout history, the Lord God continued to watch over His promises to Abraham. He would establish His kingship through the tribe of Judah. On his deathbed, Jacob prophesied over his son Judah a significant Old Testament messianic prophecy. Through the laying on of his hands, Jacob declared the tribe of Judah to be the ruling tribe over all the tribes of Israel.

> Judah, you are he whom your brothers shall praise. Your hand shall be on the neck of your enemies; Your father's children shall bow down before you
>
> Genesis 49:8.

> The scepter shall not depart from Judah nor a lawgiver from between his feet until Shiloh comes. And to Him shall be the obedience of the people
>
> Genesis 49:10.

The future king of Israel would be praised by his countrymen as their ruler, lawgiver and mighty warrior whose hand shall be on the neck of their enemies. The sceptre of righteousness would not depart from the tribe of Judah. (*Shebet* Strong's # 7626 a Hebrew noun that denotes a rod, staff, club, sceptre as a mark of authority and a symbol of conquest). The dominion of Judah's lawgivers and princes would not depart until Shiloh comes. Who is Shiloh? (*Shiloh* Strong's #7886 a proper name or a title a messianic designation of Jesus. The lawgivers and the princes would not depart from the tribe of Judah until "to whom dominion belongs" comes.)[75]

In His set time, the Lord appointed His king from the house of Jesse, the Bethlehemite, who inherited the legacy of Ruth who was joined in marriage to Boaz, her redeemer kinsman. Samuel was sent by the Lord to the house of Jesse in Bethlehem, Judah to anoint for Himself a king and a man after His own heart. He would be one who would love and obey Him with all his whole heart, with all his soul, and with all his strength according to His command in Deuteronomy 6:5. While inspecting them, Samuel bypassed all of Jesse's elder sons:

---

[75] Jack W. Hayford, *New Spirit-Filled Life Bible: Kingdom Equipping Through the Power of the Word*. (Nashville, Tennessee: Thomas Nelson, Inc., 2002) 70.

For the Lord does not see as man sees, for man looks at the outward appearance, but the Lord looks at the heart   I Samuel 16:7.

There remained yet the youngest and there he is keeping the sheep. And Samuel said to Jesse, 'Send and bring him' So he sent and brought him in. Now he was ruddy with bright eyes and good looking. And the Lord said, "Arise anoint him for this is the one"   I Samuel 16:11-13.

Samuel was not impressed or moved by the outward appearance of Jesse's elder sons. However, Jesse had one more son, David who was watching over his sheep. When Samuel saw David, the Lord said, "Arise anoint him this is the one." David was the one who would be the shepherd watching over the sheep of Israel, a mighty conqueror of surrounding enemy nations, and the king who would lead His people in a joyous and glorious worship, exalting the Lord their God in Jerusalem!

Today, the Lord God and Father is searching for true worshippers who worship Him in spirit and truth. "But the hour is coming, and now is when the true worshippers will worship the Father in spirit and truth, for the Father is seeking such to worship Him." (John 4:23) The true worshippers are like King David. They seek to know Him intimately and love Him with their whole heart. His people will have a heart to love and obey Him keeping His commandments. His vision is to create for Himself a one new humanity who will answer His call to enter into His royal priesthood and advance His Kingdom on earth as it is in heaven! What can one learn from King David?

Kathleen Martinez

David a Skillful Player, Mighty Man of Valor a Man of War

When David was anointed by Samuel, the Spirit of the Lord came upon him from that day forward. At the same time, the Spirit of the Lord departed from Saul, and an evil spirit fell upon him terrifying him. (*baath* Strong's # 1204 a Hebrew verb (Piel) denoting to fall upon, startle, terrify). Because Saul refused to submit to himself to the rule of God, he was no longer under His protective covering and became vulnerable to the control of an evil spirit. Seeing the king in distress, his servants suggested that they would seek a musician, a skillful player, who would relieve him of the oppressive spirit. One servant had seen a son of Jesse "who was skillful in playing, a mighty man of valor, a man of war, prudent in speech, and a handsome person and the Lord is with him" (I Samuel 16:18).

Upon hearing about David, the son of Jesse, Saul sent his servants to bring him into his presence. When David stood before him, the king showed him great favor. Moreover, the king loved him and appointed him as his armorbearer. Whenever an evil spirit came upon Saul, David, a skilful minstrel, would take his harp and play it. Through his worship, David would bring down the presence of the Lord, causing the evil spirit to depart from Saul. As David created an atmosphere of praise and worship, Saul would feel refreshed. (*nagan* Strong's # 5059 Hebrew verb denotes to touch strings, to play a stringed instrument,(a *kinnowr* Strong's #3658) with his hand. Furthermore, as David played the harp with his hand, David was waging warfare, thrusting and driving out the evil spirit.

Through his cunning great skill, David was not only a gifted worshipper; he was mighty warrior who would prove himself in the presence of the army of Israel. It came to pass that a Philistine by the name of Goliath approached and defied the army of Israel.

Determined to take action against this taunting giant, David went before Saul and offered to fight and defeat him. Saul responded to David saying, "You are not able to go against this Philistine to fight with him, for you are a youth." However, David was fully convinced that he was able to bring down the Philistine in the Name of the Lord, accomplishing a resounding victory for the army of Israel. As a young shepherd, he had been guarding his father's sheep. When a lion or a bear took a lamb out of the flock, he would grab hold of its beard, struck and killed it. As a result, David possessed strong faith in the Lord. He was not presumptuous, but held onto his confidence in the Lord his God who had delivered him from lions and bears. Facing Goliath, David was not afraid of the Philistine who was fully armed with a sword, a spear, and a javelin. As he approached this giant who was bullying him as just a boy, David boldly declared, "But I come to you in the Name of the Lord of hosts, the God of the armies of Israel whom you have defied" (I Samuel 17:45). David had selected five smooth stones from a brook, and selected one of them as his weapon. When he slung it with his sling, it struck the Philistine in his forehead and he fell to the ground. Then David cut his head off with the Philistine's sword. With the same hands that struck the harp driving away evil spirits, David thrust a stone that penetrated into the head of Goliath. He brought him down declaring, "Then this assembly shall know that the Lord does not save with sword and spear; for the battle is the Lord's and He will give you, (the giant) into our hands" (I Samuel 17:47).

Today, as demonic spirits attack the church, His mighty warriors are able to withstand them in the Name of the Lord who fights her battles. Men and women and young children have the power to overcome the enemy. They hear the story about the young warrior, David, who had faith and confidence in the Lord to defeat all of His enemies. They shall not be intimidated by the stature of their Goliath for the Lord is with them. In the same fearless spirit, Men and women of faith are willing to face persecution, and take a courageous stand for the Kingdom of God. What do they utilize

Kathleen Martinez

as weapons? They defeat the enemy with spiritual weapons of high praises, energetic worship, fervent prayer, and ongoing intercession, holding onto the shield of faith, wielding the Sword of His Spirit which is the Word of God (Ephesians 6:17) The Name of the Lord God is glorified and magnified! "Let God arise and His enemies be scattered. Let those who hate Him flee before Him... Great is the company of those who proclaimed it" (Psalm 68:1, 11). Through the unlimited power of the Spirit and the authority of His Word, His people are the great company who proclaim their victory through their risen Lord and Savior, Jesus Christ, putting Satan under their feet! Through the Name of the Lord, His army is now able to take full dominion and authority over their adversaries. "The Kingdom of God suffers violence but the violent take it by force." (Matthew 11:12) His church demonstrates the power of God by healing the sick, casting out demons, raising the dead. Through the Spirit of the Lord who is revealed through His people,the Kingdom of God is here now on earth as it is in heaven.(Matthew 12:28)

For over sixty years, principalities, powers and rulers of darkness and spiritual hosts of wickedness in heavenly places have built up strongholds, attempting to undermine the faith of the American church. While the church has fallen asleep, corrupt men and women have gained power and authority. Ruling in high places, they have accomplished their evil agenda of tearing down kingdom culture and values here in America and around the world. Through their progressive propaganda, the media, justices of high courts, politicians, celebrities, and educated elite have persuaded many young people to abandon their faith in God and embrace secular worldview. Moreover, they advocate compromising the truth in favor of a variety of corrupt belief systems that directly conflict with the truth of the Gospel of the Kingdom. Good is evil and evil is good. Instead of regarding the sacredness of human life, abortion has become the woman's right to choose. She may end the life of her unborn child. Furthermore, the ideology of the separation of church and state now threatens to eradicate religious liberty and establish an atheistic socialistic state ruled by wealthy elites who rob the average Americans of their wealth and well being imposing an excise of high taxes. Now the creation of these oppressive humanitarian policies are the result of the church of America turning away from God, refusing to stand up for their faith and civil rights under the Constitution. In order to save America, the church must awaken from her slumber, seek the Lord with humility and brokenness, and repent from her sin and apathy.

> If My people, who are called by My Name, humble themselves and pray and seek My face, repent, and turn from their wicked ways, then I will hear from heaven, and will forgive their sin, and heal their land.   II Chronicles 7:14

The Lord is waiting for His people to return back to Him and enter into a covenantal relationship with Him. When they fall in love with the Lord Jesus Christ, they will bring heaven down to earth participating as His co-laborers with the Spirit of the Lord in the end time harvest. (Matthew 24:14) When His people exhibit His unconditional love and show mercy for the lost, they are proclaiming the Gospel of His Kingdom to all nations so that His glory will cover the earth as the waters cover the sea. The lost are drawn unto the Kingdom of God by a demonstration of His loving kindness. Many souls are longing for the unconditional love of the Father who is calling His army to reach out and respond to the inner cry of lost humanity for unconditional love, grace, and compassion.

The Spirit of God desires to take hold of the hearts of His saints so that they recognize that this is the season for them to take a stand for the Kingdom of God and in intercessory prayer bind the demonic spirits that control leaders in high places of influence. He is calling them to battle against the forces of evil so that the Spirit of truth and righteousness will prevail against divisive leaders who organize unruly mobs. Their outrageous behavior is under the control of demonic spirits of hate, murder, and intolerance against God and His church.

However, the gates of hell shall not prevail against the church. In his letter to the Ephesians, Paul exhorts his brethren:

> Be strong in the Lord, and in the power of His might. Put on the whole armor of God that you may be able to stand against the wiles of the devil. For we do not wrestle against flesh and blood, but against principalities, against powers, against rulers of the darkness of this age, against spiritual hosts of wickedness in the heavenly places. Therefore take up the whole armor of God that you may be able to withstand in the evil day, and having done all to stand"   Ephesians 6:10-13.

They do not fight against human beings, but are battling the dark forces of evil in heavenly places. Since they are seated together with "Christ at the right hand in heavenly places far above all principality,(rule), power(authority), might and dominion" (Ephesians 1:20,21)[76] From a position of supreme power and authority, the saints stand against hate, injustice, and oppression. Moreover, they are to rule and reign with Christ now on earth willing to take on leadership in all public places in America including media, entertainment, sports, health care, education, economics, and politics. The church is to bear the responsibility of electing godly men and women into public office, and interceding for them in fervent prayer. Moreover, they support godly ministries with their prayers of intercession in the Spirit, spiritual wealth and power. Now, let them exercise dominion and power that Christ has given back to the church. Jesus came and

---

[76] Jack W. Hayford, *New Spirit-Filled Life Bible: Kingdom Equipping Through the Power of the Word.* (Nashville, Tennessee: Thomas Nelson, Inc., 2002), 1646.

spoke to them, "All authority has been given to Me in heaven and on earth" (Matthew 28:18)

Over 200 years ago, the United States Constitution was written and signed by the founding fathers to protect and defend the freedom and prosperity of a moral republic ruled by law. However, the church has allowed laws passed by Congress and decisions handed down by Supreme Court Justices which directly oppose the moral laws of God and Kingdom values. The cry of Spirit of God is for the church to break off the yoke of bondage hanging over America and put an end to divisive rulers who have created a spirit of disunity and hatred. Today, the church is called to advance and expand the Kingdom of God. His Spirit of truth, love, and unity in the church is to be the greatest weapon against the demonic deceptive forces that cause division and violence. The unity of the church is to be centered on her faith in the Lord Jesus Christ pursuing peace and love for one another. Moreover, Christians are not to engage in heated theological disputes. "Avoid foolish and ignorant disputes knowing that they generate strife" (II Timothy 2:23).

Under the anointing of the Spirit of God, the saints of God are to be like David who conquered and triumphed over all his enemies. Then, he established Jerusalem as the political, cultural, and religious center of Israel. In a spirit of rejoicing, King David led His people in a dynamic and energetic display of praise and worship of Yahweh the Almighty Sovereign Lord God in Jerusalem, achieving political and spiritual unity of the twelve tribes of Israel.

The Annointing of David
as King Over Israel

At Hebron, David's reign over all of Israel was firmly established when he made a covenant with all the tribes of Israel before the Lord. They anointed him as their King (II Samuel 5). David began his reign of forty years at the age of thirty. With his mighty men, the king conquered and seized Jerusalem and renamed it the City of David establishing it as his military, political, and religious cultural center forever.

> And the king and his men went up to Jerusalem against the Jebusites, the inhabitants of the land who spoke to David saying "You shall not come up here; but the blind and the lame will repel you thinking, "David cannot come in here." Nevertheless, David took the stronghold of Zion (that is the City of David). So David went on and became great and the Lord of Hosts was with him.
>
> II Samuel 5:5-8, 10.

David was able to conquer the Jebusites and take the stronghold of Zion that he renamed the City of David because the Lord of Hosts was with him. He was a great and mighty warrior of renown. When the Philistines heard that David was anointed to be king over Israel, they went up to defeat him in battle. David inquired of the Lord if he should go up against the Philistines. Would they be delivered into his hand? In His response, the Lord assured him victory. "Go up, for I will doubtless deliver the Philistines into your hand" (II Samuel 5:19).

In II Samuel 6, King David decided to bring up the Ark of God to Jerusalem and set up the City of David as the cultic center of Israel. The Ark of God, the very Presence of God, was called by the Name, the Lord of Hosts who dwelt between the cherubim (guardian angels Exodus 25:18). On the appointed day of celebration, David gathered his choice men of Israel to Jerusalem. He placed the Ark of God on a new cart. As King David and all the house of Israel were rejoicing and playing musical instruments before the Lord, the oxen began to stumble. Immediately, Uzzah, one of the priests, put forth his hand to stabilize the Ark. However, this irreverent action aroused the anger of the Lord. God struck him and he died. On that day, David was angry and afraid of the Lord. He realized that no one was to touch the Ark, showing disrespect for His presence. Therefore, he moved the Ark to the house of a Levite named Obed-Edom where it remained for three months until he found the proper way to transport it. According to the Law of Moses, the children of the Levites bore the Ark of God on their shoulders by its poles (I Chronicles 15:15).[77] Today, the highest calling of the church is to bear the Presence of the Lord and transform society!

Finally, the day came when David removed the ark of God from the house of Obed-Edom and brought His Presence into the City of David. In a festive atmosphere, the Levites now carried the Ark bearing it on their shoulders. At every six paces of the Levites, oxen and fatted sheep were sacrificed. David began to dance (*karar* Strong's # 3769 to whirl) with all his might girding himself with linen ephod, wearing a priestly garment ('*ephowd* Strong's #646 shoulder cape or white mantle). The king was shouting along with the sound of the trumpet (II Samuel 6:14, 15). From the window of the palace, Michal observed her husband leaping and whirling. As the daughter of Saul, she despised him in heart. After offering burnt offerings and peace offerings, David blessed the people in the Name of the Lord. Then he returned to bless his house. In a critical spirit,

---

[77] Jack W. Hayford, *New Spirit-Filled Life Bible: Kingdom Equipping Through the Power of the Word.* (Nashville, Tennessee: Thomas Nelson, Inc., 2002) 409.

Kathleen Martinez

Michal attacked and ridiculed David, with a sharp tongue saying, "How glorious was the king of Israel today, uncovering himself in the eyes of the maids, his servants as one of the base fellows shamelessly uncovered himself" (II Samuel 6:20). In response, David reminded his wife that the Lord had chosen him instead of her father ... appointed him ruler over the people of the Lord over Israel." Therefore, in a spirit of pure joy and ecstasy, he declared that he will continue to play music before the Lord and be more undignified and humble in his own sight. Like an exuberant child, celebrating without shame before the presence of his heavenly Father, David danced with a carefree spirit, having no concern about the criticisms of others. Because Michael had a bitter spirit toward her husband, the Lord disallowed her to bear children. David began to recognize that the Lord had made him king of Israel. Among all nations, he acquired a great name and enjoyed rest from all his enemies. Now David desired in his heart to build a house for the ark of God. However, the Lord wanted to build an everlasting house for David.

The Establishment of the Davidic Covenant

> I took you from the sheepfold, from following sheep, to be ruler over My people, over Israel. And I have been with you wherever you have gone, and have cut off all your enemies from before you, and I have made you a great name, like the name of the great men who are on the earth. Moreover, I will appoint a place for My people Israel, and I will plant them that they may dwell in a place of their own and move no more; nor shall the sons of wickedness oppress them anymore.   II Samuel 7:8-10

When God made David ruler over God's people, Israel was to be planted in the land, an appointed place that the Lord God had promised to Abraham and his descendents as their inheritance forever (Genesis 12:7; 13:14-17; 15:7). Israel would dwell in her own land and remain there having a sense of security, peace, and rest. She would move no more nor be under the oppressive rule of wicked men. Israel would be ruled forever under the house of David as an everlasting dynasty.

> The Lord tells you that He will make you a house. When your days are fulfilled and you rest with your fathers, I will set up a seed after you who will come from your body, and I will establish his kingdom. He shall build a house for My Name.
>
> And I will establish the throne of his kingdom forever. I will be his Father and he shall be My son. If he commits iniquity, I will chasten him with the

rod of men and with the blows of the sons of men. But My mercy shall not depart from him as I took it from Saul whom I removed from before you.

And your house and your kingdom shall be established forever before you. Your throne shall be established forever.   II Samuel 7:11-16.

After the days of David were fulfilled and he rested with his forefathers, Solomon, his son, arose as king and built a house for the Name of the Lord God of Israel. (I Kings 6:11-14). Upon the house that Solomon built, the Lord placed His Name and consecrated it for His glory. However, Solomon was to be like his father David, who walked before the Lord in the integrity of his heart and in uprightness, to do all that the Lord commanded him, to keep His statutes, and His judgments long as Israel was faithful to her covenant with the Lord God. If Solomon or his sons turned away from following the Lord...and go and serve other gods and worship them, then He would cut off Israel from the land which He gave them and the house consecrated for His Name would be cast out of His sight (I Kings 9: 4-7).

The Fall of Jerusalem took place because the leaders and the people transgressed more and more according to all the abominations of the nations and defiled the house of the Lord which He had consecrated in Jerusalem. The Lord God sent warnings to His people by His messengers because He had compassion on them. But they mocked the messengers of God, despised His words, and scoffed at His prophets until the wrath of the Lord arose against them till there was no remedy. (II Chronicles 36:14-15) (*marpe* Strong's # 4832 restoration of health, remedy, cure, medicine, tranquility, deliverance, salvation.) [78]

Under the law of the Old Covenant, the sacrifices offered were

---

[78] Jack W. Hayford, *New Spirit-Filled Life Bible: Kingdom Equipping Through the Power of the Word.* (Nashville, Tennessee: Thomas Nelson, Inc., 2002) 1273.

a reminder of sins every year. For it was not possible that the blood of bulls and goats could take away sins. Therefore, a new and better covenant would have to be established (Jeremiah 31:31-33; Hebrews 10:1, 3, 4).

Living Under the New Covenant Appendix A

Behold, the days are coming, says the Lord, when I will make a new covenant with the house of Israel and with the house of Judah— not according to the covenant that I made with their fathers in the day when I took them by the hand to lead them out of the land of Egypt, because they did not continue in My covenant, and I disregarded them, says the Lord.

For this is the covenant that I will make with the house of Israel after those days, says the Lord: I will put my laws in their mind and will write them on their hearts; and I will be their God, and they shall be My people.

None of them shall teach his neighbor, and none his brother, saying' Know the Lord,' for all shall know me from the least of them to the greatest of them. For I will be merciful to their unrighteousness, and their sins and their lawless deeds I will remember no more.

Hebrews 8:8-12 and Hebrews 10: 16, 17.

For what purpose does the writer of Hebrews refer back to the Old Testament prophecy of Jeremiah? Who is his audience? He is writing to the earliest Christians predominately Jewish who were facing severe persecutions hoping for the immediate return of Christ.[79]

---

[79] Jack W. Hayford, *New Spirit-Filled Life Bible: Kingdom Equipping Through the Power of the Word.* (Nashville, Tennessee: Thomas Nelson, Inc., 2002) 1728.

When His return is delayed, the writer exhorts them to remain steadfast in their faith in the midst of their trials and tribulations. Although they had been plundered of their earthly possessions, they have an assurance of "a better and enduring possession in heaven". "Therefore, do not cast away your confidence which has great reward" (Hebrews 10:34, 35)

Following the example of Old Testament saints whose names are recorded in the eleventh chapter of Hebrews, they must continue to endure, placing their full confidence in Christ, their promised Redeemer, believing for the salvation of their souls. Since the beginning of time in human history, the Holy Scriptures has exonerated men and women of faith have proven to be heroic in their steadfast loyalty to the Lord. They remain faithful, standing on His "great and precious promises through these you may be partakers of the divine nature having, escaped the corruption that is in the world through lust" (II Peter 1:4).

Today there is a race of faith set before all true men and women of faith. The writer of Hebrews declares all believers who are in the race of faith "must lay aside every weight and the sin which so easily ensnares and run with endurance the race that is set before them" (Hebrews 12:1). It is essential that all believers repent, turn away, and renounce any sin or hindrance that may hold them back from running the race with endurance. For those who are humble and contrite, the grace of God extends His unconditional forgiveness and healing (II Chronicles 7:14).

Under the New Covenant that was established by the Blood of Jesus, sins are forgiven. " This cup is the new covenant in My Blood which is shed for you" (Luke 22:20) Now, they enter into a personal relationship with God who puts His laws in their minds and writes them on their hearts so that they can be His people and He is their God. Ezekiel 36:25-29, reveals the work of the Holy Spirit of God. He washes His people with water. "to cleanse them from all their filthiness and their idols." Then He gives them a new heart and a new spirit within. He removes the stony heart and replaces it with a devoted heart that desires to love Him and obey His commandments. Moreover, He puts His Spirit within them to cause them to "walk in His statutes and to keep His judgments so that they may dwell in the land that He gave to their fathers. "They shall be My people and I will be their God"

Upon the receiving of their salvation, the Holy Spirit washes His people "through the washing of regeneration and the renewing of the Holy Spirit" (Titus 3:5) (*anakainosis A* Greek word Strong's #342 denoting renovation, restoration, transformation, and a change of heart through the work of the Holy Spirit). According to Paul in Romans 8:1-2, the Spirit of God removes all condemnation. "There is, therefore, now no condemnation for those who are in Christ Jesus who walk not according to the flesh, but according to the Spirit. For the Law of the Spirit of Life in Christ Jesus has made me free from the law of sin and death." Under the New Covenant, new believers are freely forgiven of all their sins. The Spirit of God enables them to walk in obedience to His Law and to keep His judgments. Doing what is right and pleasing in His eyes, His people glorify Him. Holy Spirit of grace and comfort is the Divine Enabler who empowers them to live up to His standards of righteousness as faithful witnesses of His salvation and as the light shining in a world of darkness.

> Arise; shine; For your Light has come! And the glory of the Lord is risen upon you. For behold, the darkness shall cover the earth and deep darkness the people; But the Lord will arise over you, And His glory will seen upon you   Isaiah 60:1, 2.

How do new believers continue to live the Christian life in an apostate society? They submit themselves to the Spirit of the Lord and allow Him to guide them in their daily lives. They learn to be sensitive to the Holy Spirit, taking heed to what He is saying in their spirit. The Holy Spirit speaks to them through the Word of God, the Holy Bible. Therefore, they must diligently study the Bible daily applying the Truth as a lamp unto their feet and a light to their path. Psalm 119:105. The Word of God guides their steps and keeps them on the right path of righteousness. In this race in order to achieve full maturity in Christ, the believers will continue to "grow in the grace and the knowledge of the Lord and Savior Jesus Christ" (II Peter 3: 18). Overall, the goal is to know Him in an intimate and personal way and enjoying a close love relationship with Him. Behold Jesus is standing at the door knocking, "If anyone hears My Voice and opens the door, I will come in to him and dine with him and he with Me" (Revelation 3:20). Nothing can replace a daily moment by moment relationship with Jesus. He wants His people to spend time with Him and get to know Him as their first love.

> Blessed is the man who listens to Me watching daily at my gates, waiting at the posts of my doors. For whoever finds Me finds life And obtains favor from the Lord. But he who sins against Me wrongs his own soul. All those who hate me love death.
>
> Proverbs 8:34-36

Anyone who turns away from Him wrongs his soul. In the end, the one who hates Jesus loves death which is eternal separation from Him in Hell. He who believes in Jesus, the only begotten Son of God will not perish but will have eternal life. He is saved and his works that are done through the Spirit of God will bring glory to God. On the other hand, the one who hates the light and refuses to come to the Light, loves darkness. For The Light exposes his evil deeds. He will remain in condemnation and face His wrath and certain judgment!

> For God so loved the world that He gave His only begotten Son that whoever believes in Him should not perish but have everlasting life. For God did

not send His Son into the world to condemn the world, but that the world through Him might be saved. He who believes in Him is not condemned; but he who does not believe is condemned already, because he has not believed in the name of the only begotten Son of God. And this is the condemnation that the light has come into the world, and men love darkness rather than light because their deeds are evil. For everyone practicing evil hates the light and does not come to the light, lest his deeds should be exposed. But he who does the truth comes to the light, that his deeds may be clearly seen that they have been done in God.   John 3:16-21

In the final statement closing the book of Hebrews, the writer issues a benediction

Now may the God of peace who brought up our Lord Jesus from the dead, that Great Shepherd of the sheep through the blood of the everlasting covenant make you complete in every good work to do His will, working in you what is pleasing in His sight, through Jesus Christ, to whom be glory forever and ever. Amen   Hebrews 13:20,21

Sons of God — Destined to Rule and Reign with Christ Appendix B

As they are led by the Spirit, they are sons of God who recognize and obey their Father's Voice. They are no longer controlled by spirit of bondage to fear. The love of the Father casts out all fear of punishment and rejection.

> For as many as are led by the Spirit of God, these are the sons of God. For you do not receive the spirit of bondage again to fear, but you received the Spirit of adoption by whom we cry out "Abba Father" The Spirit bears witness with our spirit that we are the children of God, and if children heirs—heirs of God and joint heirs with Christ, if indeed we suffer with Him, that we may also be glorified together.
>
> Romans 8:14-17.

As they receive the Spirit of adoption by whom, they cry out "Abba Father". The Spirit reveals to their spirit that they are not only the children of God, but are joint heirs with Christ if they are willing to suffer with Him. Through their suffering in Christ, they reveal the glory of God to all the nations.

All who are godly will have to endure a short time of persecution on earth suffering for Christ. But, whoever suffers for Christ will also be glorified together with Him forever.

> How do they endure living in such uncertain times? They look unto Jesus, the author and the finisher of their faith. Jesus endured the cross despising the

Kathleen Martinez

shame, and has sat down at the right hand of the
throne of God.   Hebrews 12:1 2.

During His passion on the cross, Christ left His people a noble
example that they can follow in His footsteps:

> Who committed no sin nor was deceit found in
> His mouth who when reviled, did not revile in
> return; when He suffered, He did not threaten, but
> committed Himself to Him who judges righteously.
>   I Peter 2:21-23

Now, the saints place their full confidence and faith in God
the Father, trusting in Him who will judge according to His
righteousness all men for their ungodly actions against them. They
are assured that Divine Justice will be done. The wicked will face the
Day of Judgment and receive punishment for what they did in this
life. "It is appointed for men to die once, but after this the judgment"
(Hebrews 9:27) All their evil actions committed against them will be
judged at the Great White Throne of Judgment. All the wicked will
be condemned and cast away into the Lake of Fire for all eternity.
(Revelation 20:11-15). On the other hand, the Redeemed of the
Lord will enter into an eternity of glory and bliss in His Presence.
Meanwhile, all of creation holds onto an earnest expectation of
the glory (*doxa* Strong's #1391 denotes the glory, the splendor, the
radiance and the majesty seen in the miracles of Christ)[80] which shall
be revealed of the sons of God.

> For I consider that the sufferings of this present time
> are not worthy to be compared with the glory which
> shall be revealed in us. For the earnest expectation

---

[80] Jack W. Hayford, *New Spirit-Filled Life Bible: Kingdom Equipping Through
the Power of the Word.* (Nashville, Tennessee: Thomas Nelson, Inc., 2002)
1446.

of creation eagerly waits for the revealing of the sons
of God.   Romans 8:18,19

Now as the sons of God, the saints await full redemption of their
bodies at the return of Jesus Christ. They are groaning in their spirit
along with all of creation, longing to be set free from the futility
of moral and physical decay caused by the increasing weight of sin
throughout human history.

> Creation was subjected to futility, not willingly, but
> because of Him who subjected it in hope; because
> the creation itself also will be delivered from the
> bondage of corruption into the glorious liberty of
> the children of God. For we know that the whole
> creation groans and labors with birth pangs together
> until now. Not only that but we also who have
> the firstfruits of the Spirit, even we ourselves groan
> within ourselves eagerly waiting for the adoption,
> the redemption of our body.   Romans 8:18-23.

Since the Fall of Adam in the Garden of Eden, the Lord God has
given hope of His deliverance from death, decay, and bondage to His
creation, promising to send forth His Redeemer (Genesis 3:15). Then
at the day of His resurrection, Christ won His glorious victory over
death, the last enemy of humanity. At His second coming, (*parousia*
Strong's # 3952) a glorious arrival of the Messiah)[81], He shall put an
end to death forever.

> But now Christ is risen from the dead and has
> become the first fruits of those who have fallen
> asleep (died).... Christ the firstfruits afterward

---

[81] Jack W. Hayford, *New Spirit-Filled Life Bible: Kingdom Equipping Through
the Power of the Word.* (Nashville, Tennessee: Thomas Nelson, Inc., 2002)
1603

Kathleen Martinez

those who are Christ's at His coming. Then
comes the end when He delivers the Kingdom
to God, the Father, when He puts an end to all
rule and all authority and power. For He must
reign till He has put all enemies under His feet.
The last enemy that will be destroyed is death

I Corinthians 15:20, 23 -26

The battle between the kingdom of Satan and the forces of
evil and the Kingdom of God has been waged throughout human
history. However, in these last days starting with the outpouring of
the Holy Spirit (Acts 2:17, Joel 2:28-32), the saints of the Most High
took possession of the Kingdom of heaven. Now the Kingdom of
heaven suffers violence and extreme opposition from the enemy, but
the violent take it by force (Matthew 11:12). The Church of Jesus
Christ is engaged in an intense warfare with the antichrist system
of this world.

And every spirit that does not confess that Jesus
Christ has come in the flesh is not of God. And this
is the spirit of Antichrist which you have heard was
coming and is now in the world. You are of God
little children and have overcome them, because He
who is in you is greater than he who is in the world

I John 4:3-4

The spirit of Antichrist opposes the reincarnation of the Son of
God. Through the indwelling Spirit of God, the children of God
are greater than the spirit of Antichrist. Therefore, they possess the
power of God to have overcome him.

Although Christ won a resounding victory over the kingdom of
Satan, the saints take possession of the Kingdom of God exercising
dominion over all of creation originally granted to humanity (Adam)
at the time of his creation (Genesis 1:26-28). The power of Satan

will be manifested in the person of the Antichrist who will speak pompous words against the Most High. He shall persecute the saints of the Most High until the Ancient of Days puts on end to his rule. All earthly kingdoms opposing the Kingdom of heaven will come to a final end, as the Son of Man comes in the clouds of heaven before the heavenly Father. He is the Ancient of Days who sits upon the throne of fire before countless worshippers who love and obey Him.

> I was watching in the night visions and Behold, One like the Son of Man Coming in the clouds of heaven. He came to the Ancient of Days. And they brought Him near before Him. Then to Him (The Father) was given dominion and glory and a kingdom that all the peoples, nations and languages should serve Him. His dominion is an everlasting dominion, which will not pass away. And His kingdom the one which will not be destroyed   Daniel 7:13, 14.

According to the vision of the prophet Daniel in Daniel 7 and the vision of John in Revelation 20:11-15, the saints will patiently endure tribulation until the end. And the God of peace will crush Satan under their feet shortly. The grace of our Lord Jesus Christ be with you. Amen. (Romans 16:20).

> The Lord Jesus Christ will be glorified in His Church that is that He might present her to Himself a glorious church not having spot or wrinkle or any such thing, but that she should be holy and without blemish.   Ephesians 5:27

How does the Bride of Christ keep herself pure and holy? She seeks Him with all her heart, not wandering away from Him, hiding His Word in her heart that she will not sin against Him. She desires to do what is pleasing in His sight out of deep love and devotion.

Kathleen Martinez

How can a young man cleanse his way? He takes heed according to Your word. With my whole heart I have sought You. Oh let me not wander from Your commandments! Your word I have hid in my heart that I might not sin against You Psalm 119:9-11.

And now little children abide in Him that when He appears, we may have confidence and not be ashamed before Him at His coming. Beloved what manner of love the Father has bestowed on us that we should be called children of God! Therefore the world does not know us, because it did not know Him Beloved, now we are the children of God and it has not yet been revealed what we shall be, but we know that when He is revealed, we shall be like Him, for we shall see Him as He is. And everyone who has this hope in Him, purifies himself just as he is pure   I John 2:28, 29; 3:1-3.

From the day of his creation Adam (humanity) was created to reflect the glory of God in manifesting His loving nature, and His holiness (pure, *Katharos* Strong's # 2513without blemish, clean, and undefiled)[82] and represent of His Kingdom of righteousness, peace and joy on earth!

Finally we know that all things work together for good to those who love God to those who are called according to His purpose (*prosthesis* purpose Strong's #4286 His eternal plan and purpose for their salvation.) For He foreknew, He also did predestinate to be conformed to the image of His

---

[82] Jack W. Hayford, *New Spirit-Filled Life Bible: Kingdom Equipping Through the Power of the Word.* (Nashville, Tennessee: Thomas Nelson, Inc., 2002) 1296.

Son, that we might be the firstborn among many
brethren.   Romans 8:28, 29

Before the foundation of the earth, The Lord God foreknew
those who would answer and respond to His call of salvation. Even
before the Lord formed Jeremiah in the womb, He knew and called
him to fulfill His plan and purpose. (Jeremiah 1:4:5) Before he was
born, the Lord set him apart and ordained him to be a prophet to the
nations. The calling of Jeremiah illustrates that God has complete
knowledge of every person and is acquainted with all his or her
ways. When the Lord views a child being formed in the womb of
his or her mother, He sees the full potential of that child to become
fully formed in His image and likeness as a child of God. And in
His book, He records all the days of his or her life. No child is
placed on earth as an accident without great value and significance
in the eyes of the heavenly Father. How precious are His thoughts
toward every one He creates. (Psalm 139:14-17) Furthermore, He
predestinates every person who responds to the call of His salvation,
to be conformed to the image of His Son. At the very moment of
spiritual rebirth the Spirit of God, He quickens and makes alive the
spirit that dwells in the innermost being of His newborn child. He
enters into eternal life (John 3:6, 15). Through the sanctifying work
of the Holy Spirit, He conforms His child to the image of His Son.
"Being confident of this very thing, that He who began a good work
in you will complete it until the day of Jesus Christ (Philippians
1:6) He patiently forms and fashions His divine nature of love and
compassion and His Holy and pure character within the heart of
the new believer, setting him or her apart unto Himself. "Come
out from among them and be separate says the Lord Do not touch
what is unclean and I will receive you. I will be a Father to you and
you shall be my sons and daughters says the Lord Almighty" (II
Corinthians 6:17, 18).

Moreover whom He predestined, these He called (*kaleo Strong's
#2564* denotes invitation to participate in the blessings of the

Kingdom of God)[83] these He also justified and whom He justified, (*dikaioo* Strongs # 1344 denotes to acquit, declare righteous on the Day of Judgment)[84] these He also glorified (Romans 8:30). Now those who have the firstfruits of the Spirit groan within themselves eagerly waiting for the adoption, the redemption of their bodies. (Romans 8:23).

> In a moment, in the twinkling of an eye, at the sound of the last trumpet. For the trumpet will sound, and the dead will be raised incorruptible, and we shall be changed. For this corruptible must put on incorruption and this mortal must put on immortality. So when this corruptible has put on incorruption, and this mortal has put on immortality, then shall be brought to pass the saying that is written, "Death is swallowed up in victory." O death where is your sting? O Hades, where is your victory? The sting of death is sin and the strength of sin is the law. But thanks be to God who gives us victory through our Lord Jesus Christ!
> I Corinthians 15:52-57.

In the meantime, sons of God are called to fulfill the Great Commission of Christ.

> And Jesus came and spoke to them, saying, "All authority has been given to Me in heaven and on earth, "Go therefore and make disciples of all nations baptizing them in the Name of the Father and of the Son and of the Holy Spirit, teaching them to observe all things that I have commanded

---

[83] Jack W. Hayford, *New Spirit-Filled Life Bible: Kingdom Equipping Through the Power of the Word.* (Nashville, Tennessee: Thomas Nelson, Inc., 2002) 1603.
[84] Ibid. 1312.

you, and lo, I am with you always, even to the end
of the age."   Matthew 28:18-20.

Go into all the world and preach the gospel to
every creature. He who believes and is baptized
will be saved; but he who does not believe will be
condemned. And these signs will follow those who
believe: In My Name, they will cast out demons;
speak in new tongues...they will lay hands on the
sick and they will recover.   Mark 16:15-18.

Along with the Great Commission, Jesus had promised to give
His disciples another Helper Comforter (*Parakletos* Strong's # 3875
para beside and *kaleo* to call to one's side an intercessor, comforter,
helper, advocate and counselor who gives strength to endure hostility
of the world system)[85]

The Spirit of Truth whom the world cannot receive,
because it neither sees Him nor knows Him; but
you know Him for He dwells with you and will be
in you. I will not leave you orphans; I will come to
you   John 14:16-18.

But you shall receive power when the Holy Spirit
has come upon you and you shall be witnesses to
Me in Jerusalem, and in Judea, and Samaria and to
the end of the earth.   Acts 1:8.

The Holy Spirit empowers the disciples of Jesus to be His
witnesses (*Martus* Strong's # 3144 one who testifies to the truth of
what he has experienced as a witness) [86]

---

[85] Ibid. 1472.
[86] Ibid. 1816.

Kathleen Martinez

Paul declares in I Corinthians 2:4 " And my speech and my preaching were not persuasive words of human wisdom, but in demonstration of the Spirit and of power, that your faith should not be in the wisdom of men but in the power of God" The Kingdom of God is not in word but in power (I Corinthians 4:20)

Thus the supernatural power and demonstration of the Holy Spirit in His witnesses bring men to faith and not by their persuasive words.

In Matthew 24, Jesus warns His disciples of signs of His coming and the end of the age : Spirit of deception will be present with false messiahs. There will be wars and rumors of wars, nation rising against nation, and kingdom against kingdom along with famines, pestilences, and earthquakes in various places. These events will be the beginning of sorrows. Disciples will face tribulation, death, and shall be hated by all nations for His Name's sake. Many false prophets will deceive those who have no love of the truth. Lawlessness will cause the love of many to grow cold. But he who endures to the end will be saved. (Matthew 24:5-13).

The Gospel of the Kingdom will be preached in the entire world as a witness to all nations, and then the end will come. All disciples and believers are called to share the Gospel of the Kingdom of God, doing good works that glorify God the Father. "Let your light so shine before men that they may see your good works and glorify your Father in heaven" (Matthew 5:16).

Bibliography

Works cited:

Brown F. S. Driver and C. Briggs. <u>The Brown-Driver-Briggs Hebrew and English Lexicon: Coded with Strong's Concordance Numbers</u>. Peabody, Massachusetts: Hendrickson Publishers, 2008.

Conner, Kevin J. & Ken Malmin. <u>The Covenants: The Key to God's Relationship With Mankind</u>. Portland, Oregon: City Bible Publishing, 1983.

Dickason, C. Fred. <u>Revised and Expanded Angels Elect & Evil</u>. Chicago: Moody Publishers, 1995.

Dillard, Raymond B. and Tremper Longman III. <u>An Introduction to the Old Testament</u>. Grand Rapids, Michigan: Zondervan, 1994.

Eban, Abba. <u>My People: The Story of the Jews New Edition</u>. New York: Behrman House Inc., 1984.

Gallups, Carl. <u>God's & Thrones: Nachash, Forgotten Prophecy & the Return of the Elohim</u>. Crane MO: Defender Publishing, 2017.

Jouon, Paul S.J. and T. Muraoka. <u>A Grammar of Biblical Hebrew Volume ll Part Three: Syntax Paradigm and Indices</u>. Roma: Editrice Pontificio Instituto Biblico, 2000.

Kaiser, Walter C. Jr. <u>The Old Testament Documents: Are They Reliable and Relevant?</u> Downers Grove, Illinois: InterVarsity Press, 2001.

Lotz, Anne Graham. I Saw the Lord: A Wake-Up Call for Your Heart. Grand Rapids, Michigan: Zondervan, 2006.

Luton, L. Grant. In His Own Words Messianic Insights into the Hebrew Alphabet. Uniontown, Ohio: Beth Tikkum Publishing, 1999.

Morford, William J. The One New Man Bible: Revealing Jewish Roots and Power. Traveler's Rest, South Carolina: True Potential Publishing, Inc., 2011.

Robertson O Palmer. The Christ of the Covenants. Phillipsburg, New Jersey: Presbyterian and Reformed Publishing Company, 1980.

Robertson, Pat. The Ten Offenses: Reclaim the Blessings of the Ten Commandments. Nashville, Tennessee: Integrity Publishers, 2004.

Ross Hugh. The Genesis Question: Scientific Advances and the Accuracy of Genesis. Colorado Springs, Colorado: NavPress Publishing Company, 1998.

Stone Perry. How a Mountain of Fire and a Rebellious Cherub Altered History in Heaven and on Earth Chronicles of the Sacred Mountain: Revealing The Mysteries of Heaven's Past, Present and Future. Cleveland, TN: Voice of Evangelism Outreach Ministries, 2015.

Ulmar, Kenneth. In His Image: An Intimate Reflection of God. New Kensington, PA.: Whitaker House, 2005.

Unger, Merrill F. Unger's Bible Dictionary. Chicago, Illinois: The Moody Press, 1971.

Additional Resources

Arterburn, Stephen. <u>Healing is a Choice: Ten Declarations That Will Transform Your Life Ten Lies That Can Prevent You From Making Them</u>. Nashville Tennessee: Thomas Nelson, 2005.

Bernis, Jonathan. <u>A Rabbi Looks at the Last Days: Surprising Insights on Israel, the End Times and Popular Misconceptions</u>. Minneapolis, Minnesota: Chosen Books, 2013.

Bernis, Jonathan. <u>A Rabbi Looks at Jesus of Nazareth: What happens When a Jewish Man Takes a Serious Look at the Life and Works of he Man who Claimed to be the Messiah</u>? Grand Rapids, Michigan: Chosen Books, 2011.

Blitz, Mark. <u>God's Day Timer</u>. Washington D.C.: WND Books, 2016.

Cahn, Jonathan. <u>The Book of Mysteries</u>. Lake Mary, Florida: Frontline 2016.

Cahn, Jonathan. <u>The Paradigm: The Ancient Blueprint that Holds the Mystery of Our Times</u> Lake Mary, Florida: Frontline 2017.

Corsi, Jerome R. <u>Killing the Deep State: The Fight to Save President Trump</u>. West Palm Beach, Florida: Humanix Books 2018.

Crabb, Larry. <u>Connecting: Healing for Ourselves and Our Relationships</u>. Nashville, Tennessee: Thomas Nelson, 1997.

Crabb, Larry. <u>Fully Alive: A Biblical Vision of Gender that Frees Men and Women to Beyond Stereotypes</u>. Grand Rapids, Michigan: Baker Books, 2013.

Fee, Gordon. <u>God's Empowering Presence: The Holy Spirit in the Letter of Paul</u>. Peabody Massachusetts: Hendrickson Publishers, Inc. 2008.

Fleming, Don. <u>Concise Bible Commentary: Clear, Simple, and Easy to Understand With Outlines, Charts and Maps</u>. Chattanooga, Tennessee: AMG Publishers. 1994.

Grenz, Stanley J. <u>Theology for the Community of God</u>. Grand rapids, Michigan: William B. Eerdmans Publishing Company, 1994.

Hayford, Jack W. Executive Editor <u>The Hayford Bible Handbook: The Complete Campanion for Spirit-Filled Bible Study</u>. Nashville, Tennessee: Thomas Nelson, 1995.

Hayford, Jack W. <u>Rebuilding the Real You: The Definitive Guide to the Holy Spirit's Work In Your Life</u>. Lake Mary, Florida: Charisma House Book Group, 2009.

Hayford, Jack W. and Rebecca Hayford Bauer. <u>Penetrating the Darkness</u>. Bloomington, MN: Chosen Books, 2001.

Horton, Stanley M. <u>The Ultimate Victory: An Exposition of the Book of Revelation</u>. Springfield, Missouri: Gospel Publishing House, 1991.

Kenneson, Philip D. <u>Life on the Vine: Cultivating the Fruit of the Spirit in Christian Community</u>. Downers Grove, Illinois: InterVarsity Books, 1999.

Kohlenberger III, John R. Ed. The NIV Interlinear Hebrew- English Old Testament: Four Volumes in One Genesis- Malachi Grand Rapids, Michigan: Regency Reference Library of Zondervan Publishing House 1987.

McReynolds, Paul R. Word Study Greek-English New Testament with Complete Concordance Carol Stream, Illinois: Tyndale House Publishers, 1999.

Robertson, O. Palmer. The Christ of the Covenants. Phillipsburg, New Jersey: Presbyterian and Reformed Publishing Company, 1980.

Robertson, Pat. The New World Order: It will Change the Way You Live. Dallas, Texas: Word Publishing, 1991.

Robertson, Pat. The Ten Offenses: Reclaim the Blessings of the Ten Commandments. Nashville, Tennessee: Integrity Publishers, 2004.

Robertson, A. T. A Harmony of the Gospels: The Standard Broadus Harmony Thoroughly Revised, Rearranged and Enlarged. San Francisco: Harper Collins Publishers, 1922.

Ross, Hugh. The Creator and the Cosmos: How the Latest Scientific Discoveries Reveal God. Covina, Ca: RTB Press, 2018.

Ross, Hugh and with Kathy Ross. Always Be Ready: A Call to Adventurous Faith. Covina, Ca: RTB Press, 2018.

Roth, Sid, The Incomplete Church: Bridging the Gap Between God's Children. Shippenburg, PA.: Destiny Image Publishers, 2007.

Santos, Bill. <u>David Friend of God</u>. Oshawa, Ontario, Canada: Published by It is Written, 2018.

Scazzero, Peter. <u>The Emotionally Healthy Church: A Strategy for Discipleship that Actually Changes Lives</u>. Grand Rapids, Michigan: Zondervan, 2010.

Seemuth, David P. <u>Romans: Spirit-Filled Life New Testament Commentary Series</u>. Nashville, Tennessee: Thomas Nelson, Inc., 2005.

Sheen, Fulton J. <u>Life of Christ</u>. New York: Image Books/Doubleday, 1958.

Stanley, Charles F. <u>When the Enemy Strikes: The Keys to Winning Your Spiritual Battles</u>. Nashville: Tennessee: Thomas Nelson, Inc. 2004.

Stone, Perry. <u>Chronicles of the Sacred Mountain; Revealing the Mysteries of Heaven's Past, Present and Future</u>. Cleveland, Tennessee: Voice of Evangelism Outreach Ministries, 2015.

Strong's, James. <u>Strong's Exhaustive Concordance of the Bible</u>. Nashville: Abingdon Press 1890.

Thayer, Joseph. <u>Thayer's Greek-English Lexicon of the New Testament: A Dictionary Coded To Strong's Exhaustive Concordance</u>. Grand Rapids, Michigan: Baker Book House. 1977.

Vine, .E. <u>Vine's Expository Dictionary of Old And New Testament Words</u>. Nashville, Tennessee: Thomas Nelson Publishers, 1997.

Yancey, Philip, <u>The Jesus I Never Knew</u>. Grand Rapids, Michigan: Zondervan, 1995.